Theatrum Anatomicum
(and Other Performance Lectures)

Pablo Helguera

Theatrum Anatomicum
(and Other Performance Lectures)

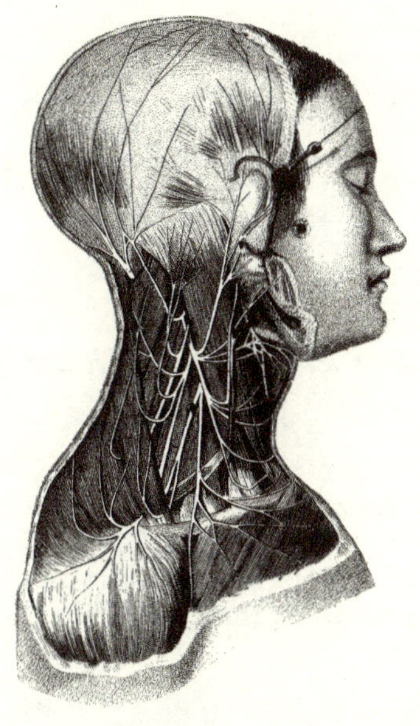

Jorge Pinto Books Inc.
New York

Theatrum Anatomicum (and Other Performance Lectures)

Cover illustration: © Pablo Helguera, *9. Actor,* from *The Seven Bridges of Königsberg,* 2008

Cover design: Susan Hildebrand / Pablo Helguera

Editor: Rebecca Roberts

Book design: Cox-King Multimedia, www.ckmm.com.

ISBN: 978-1-934978-16-0
1-934978-16-7

Contents

Ladies and Gentlemen

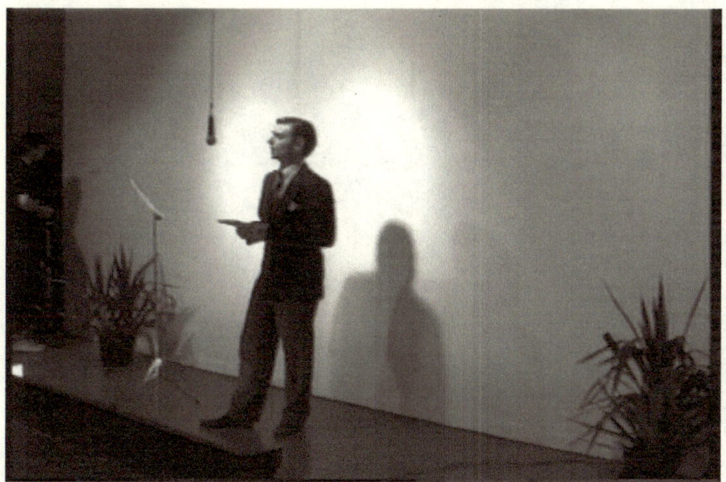

Pablo Helguera performing *Babel*, Gallery 2, Chicago, October 8, 1993

I presented my first performance lecture, unaware that such a format existed, as an art student at the School of the Art Institute of Chicago on October 8, 1993. The piece, entitled *Babel*, was my attempt to make sense of my cultural displacement from Mexico City, which I had left four years before. The work was constructed around a 1943 photograph that was the only historical connection between Chicago and me: the visit of the president of Rotary International (based in Chicago) to Mexico City, commemorated at a breakfast hosted by my grandfather (who was president of the Mexico City chapter of the club at the time). In *Babel* I made a case for the reconstruction of the photographic scene to mark the fiftieth anniversary of this otherwise banal incident. My father, who is pictured in the original photograph, became the living link to the new one, fifty years later. Those who participated in the 1993 reconstruction were told to keep in touch, because the photograph will be reconstructed again fifty years from that day, in 2043.

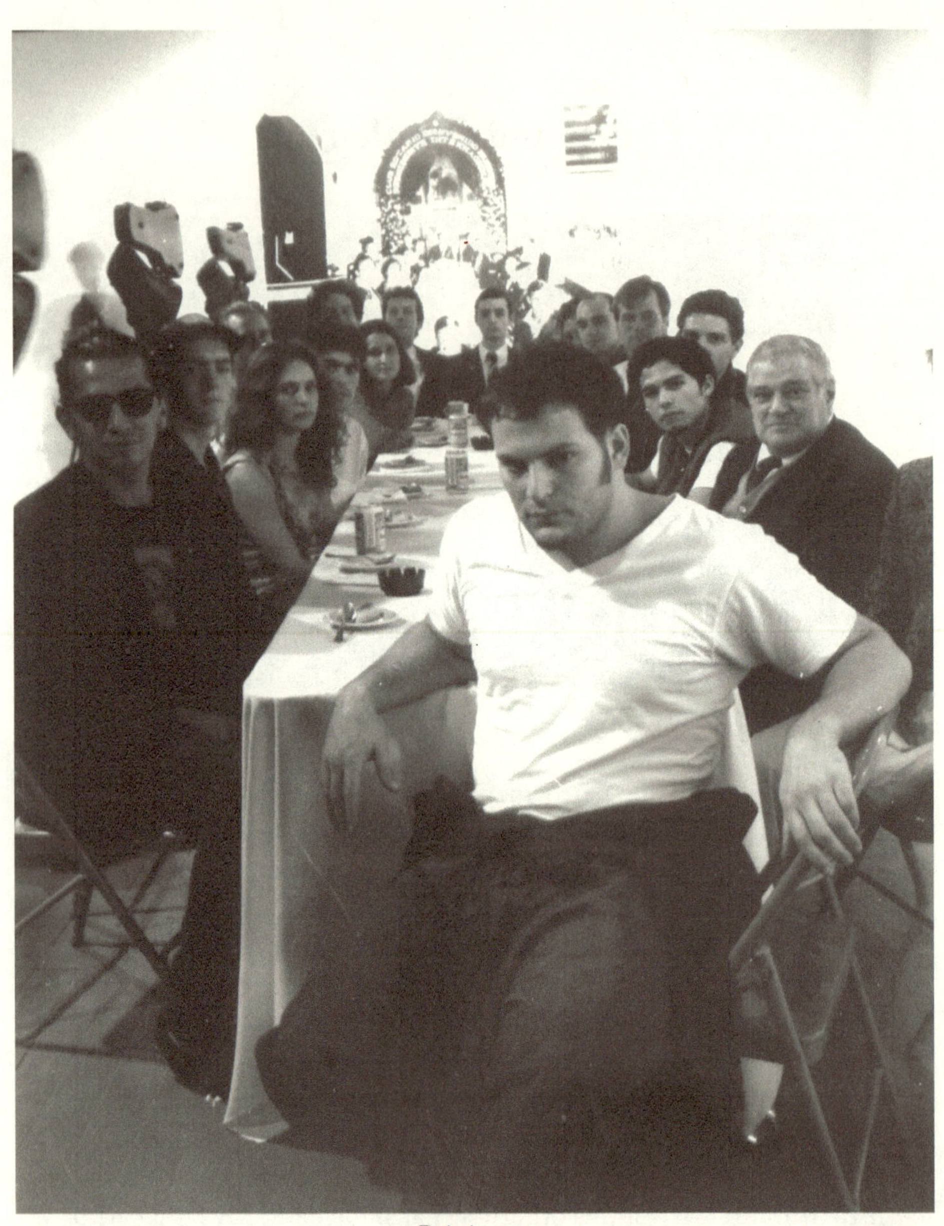

Babel, 1993

At the time, I was entirely oblivious to the legacy of Marcel Broodthaers, the work of Michael Asher, or the performative docent tours of Andrea Fraser, who had made *Museum Highlights* a few years before. Nonetheless, these decidedly postmodern experimentations with academic fiction were "in the air," and I had most definitely inhaled them. As a student I had been impacted by the work of Catalan photographer Joan Fontcuberta, who was known for his photographic fabrications of natural and scientific stories. Shortly afterward, while working as an intern in a museum, I was recruited to act as a fake museum guard/docent in the Field Museum of Natural History, Chicago, for Guillermo Gómez-Peña and Coco Fusco's performance *The Couple in the Cage*—a work that consisted of the display in a cage of two recently "discovered" Amerindians, surrounded with patronizing anthropological descriptions of these "specimens." Guillermo and Coco were inside the cage, performing, while another performer and I "explained" to outraged viewers why there were two human beings inside a cage. It was the height of the identity-politics era, and while I remained distant from the self-righteousness that much angry political art exuded at that time, I was definitely captivated by its strategies and sought to make use of them. If anything, *Babel* was a small preamble to what would become my constant interests: the analysis and fabrication of history, museum narratives, the role of fiction in the visual arts, social rituals, and so forth.

Over the last few years, the performance lecture has become a rather ubiquitous genre on the stages of highbrow museums and Brooklyn stand-up bars. Yet, as I realized while putting this collection of texts together, there is not a great deal of writing that discusses the nature and structure of the genre. This absence of a theoretical framework is somewhat liberating, because once something is theorized, it starts to get trapped in philosophical premises. But for this book I feel I have to define for myself, even if tentatively, what a performance lecture is—a task that has not yet been imposed upon me, despite the fact that I have doing such lectures since that evening in Chicago in 1993.

The easy definition of a performance lecture is that it is a live presentation imparted by an artist who takes advantage of his or her artistic license and of the conventions of academic pedagogy to create a work that straddles fiction and reality. Irony and sometimes satire are central to the event: those who attend a performance lecture generally expect an irreverent take on academicism—a trait that explains this genre's natural connection to institutional critique. Like other hybrid art genres, its very name illustrates the awkward juxtaposition of two modes of speaking that never entirely blend, much as prose poetry draws on the qualities of two different modes of writing without being entirely one or the other. Yet beyond these few points, performance lectures don't follow many rules, and like performance, the genre is in a constant process of self-definition, sometimes delving into stand-up comedy, poetic presentations, recitals, speeches, etc.

My work in museum education, begun in 1992 and continuing to this day, has required me to reflect constantly on the relationship between performativity and pedagogy that is inherent to performance lectures. Because of my involvement with performance and theater, I gravitated toward the public-programs area of museums—an area that for many years has been in serious need of revitalization. The lecture format, a seemingly necessary medium of communication and a vital staple of academia, is constantly reviled and declared dead today, and for good reasons. Ever since the publication of Donald A. Bligh's *What's the Use of Lectures?* in 1971, there has been a general awareness of the limitations of this educational format and yet very little done to innovate on it. Through the work of Bligh and others, we have repeatedly received proof that it is ineffective as a discussion method for promoting thought and that at best it is just as effective as other formats in transmitting information, yet we continue to use this presentation format that comes to us from the eighteenth century, a time when pedagogy consisted entirely of exposition and memorization. The limitations of this method become clearest with the practice of a "read paper"—usually consisting of a poorly delivered, hard-to-assimilate piece of writing that is best read at home by oneself. Academics who attend art conferences deride even their own presentations as boring and excessively long but continue to perpetuate this archaic model.

However, I believe that exasperation toward the traditional lecture format has finally reached the inner depths of the academic world, and in blogs and magazines, the lecture as we know it has been declared dead. A new type of lecture, the metalecture or lecture 2.0, must take its place.

In my role as programmer, I have frequently been frustrated by the low or nonexistent public-speaking skills of those who lecture and participate in academic discussions. While featured speakers usually have something relevant to say (which is what prompts an invitation to speak), very few of them are skilled public speakers or comfortable in a public forum, which translates into stiffness and social awkwardness, insincerity, and a general reluctance to open up toward an audience. Because most lectures are based on a written text, their unfolding is slow and their language excessively formal and heavy for a live reading. Wouldn't it be great, I thought, if panels were like theater works, where drama has its hand in conveying the message? I thought, why aren't there dramaturges for art lecturers?—and I set out to become one.

Starting in about 1998 I started scripting stand-alone performance lectures. This eventually led to the incorporation of actors in symposia and panel discussions, which I first attempted in 2003 in collaboration with artist Ilana Boltvinik with *The First Mexico City Congress of Urban Purification*, and then again in 2004 at *The First Imaginary Forum of Mental Sculpture* at the Sculpture Center in Long Island City, Queens—both texts are included in this book. Not revealing the fact that actors were "interpreting" the papers and debates was key to maintaining the audience's engagement without triggering the dismissal of the piece as yet another performance work. *We All Are Streeter* (2006), also included here, employed a similar theatrical strategy.

Another trait of the traditional lecture format that interests me is the narrowness of thematic focus that often results from the demands of scholarship. While extremely specialized topics are the logical result of academic-type research, their presentation in the shape of a lecture before a general audience can be alienating and, even if comprehensible, leaves the general spectator questioning the larger relevance of the subject at hand. This issue has become more and more aggravated because while the lecture remains set in its traditional presentation style, twenty-first-century auditoriums are filled with a new generation of viewers whose brains are wired for multichannel experiences and are capable of processing the daily deluge of information that technology now provides. Symposia and panel discussions are better opportunities for comparing perspectives on a given subject, but the patience and focus needed to sit through, say, a six-hour symposium, can only be mastered by diehards, in the same way that only an opera aficionado would sit through the entire *Götterdämmerung*. The slowness of the traditional academic lecture became even more apparent as the Internet and the digital revolution took hold. In this era of pingbacks and multichannel viewing and processing, it is normal that the most animated discussions take place online instead of in actual physical spaces. This was the motivation for works like *Theatrum Anatomicum* (P.S.1 Contemporary Art Center, New York, 2002) where I experimented with multichannel, "dueling" lectures about topics that were at first sight completely unrelated (such as twentieth-century Mexican *telenovelas* and seventeenth-century Dutch anatomical theaters) in order to shed light on both subjects and onto a larger umbrella topic.

In 2003 I was invited to perform at The Museum of Modern Art, in New York. The performance, *Parallel Lives*, was a union of sorts of my projects, including a few performance lectures, such as *Mock Turtle* (2001) (not included in this book because it was partially subsumed into *Parallel Lives*), that focused on the biographies of individuals about whom I had made exhibition projects and who I felt had much in common. *Parallel Lives* was a more complex proposition than *Theatrum Anatomicum*, based in my interest in musical composition and particularly in the desire to make a thematic and visual fugue of the biographies of the antiheroic protagonists. The work was a reflection, from the standpoint of the visual arts, on the historically omniscient and detached narrative voice of the biographer, ranging from John Aubrey's gossipy *Brief Lives* from the 1690s to the fiction-grounded *Imaginary Lives*, by Marcel Schwob, published in 1898. What attracted me in the traditional biographical voice was its similarity to the anonymous educational voice of the academic institution, and in using it I wanted to create an interpretive structure with an air of historical certainty in the references it drew and yet which left open all sorts of cracks between images and characters for the audience to fill in on their own.

In a way, *Parallel Lives* was a project about otherness and idealism—two concepts very much on my mind in the years after 9/11, the era of "the war on terror." Cynicism and alienation had become dominating cultural forces, and I found it hard not to address them in some manner. This was the leitmotif of *The Foreign Legion*, presented at the Performa 05 biennial in New York in 2005. The work merged the thematic counterpoint of *Parallel Lives* and the theatrical modalities of the fictional scholarly forums, presenting three simultaneous panel discussions with entirely different topics (one about religion, another about psychology, and yet another about a war-themed opera) that merged at the end. This continued in several other works, including *Manifest Destiny* (2008–9), which in a way brings the reflections of the previous work to a kind of closure.

Several performance lectures, such as *We All Need a Pygmalion* (2005), which is the performance version of *The Pablo Helguera Manual of Contemporary Art Style* (2005), and the speeches connected to the project *The School of Panamerican Unrest* (2006) are not included here, because those texts vary somewhat in form from the current selection: the works grouped in this book are all based on written scripts. This eliminated other works in more open formats, such as *The Symposium* (2004)—a live reconstruction of Plato's classic text of the same name. The performance took place in Rincón, Puerto Rico, and each speaker was asked to familiarize himself or herself with the philosophical outlook of one of the characters in Plato's original text, which is a debate of the nature of love, and update those positions in an argument for the love of art. The event, which included the speakers Xandra Eden, James Elkins (as Plato), Christine Hill, Ryan Hill, Nelson Rivera, Hamza Walker, and myself as the host (Agathon), was very long and joyful, fueled with food and drink as in the original Greek event.

Two main difficulties arose in bringing these live events to the printed page: the first one is in clarifying the intentional ambiguity between the scripted character and the actual lecturer or performer, which varied somewhat in every piece. For example, in some cases performers were asked to play their real-life selves, albeit with scripted material, thus blurring the boundaries between their real and their stage identities. For clarification, at the beginning of every text there is a general description of the context of the performance and the role that each speaker played. Second, many of these lectures included a full sequence of images (usually projected) that directly related to the narration. It is not possible to include here every slide used, but there are a few reference images inserted in the text to give a general sense of the role pictures played in that presentation.

It would take several pages to name all the actors and artists who participated in these projects, to all of whom I owe gratitude for their dedication and support. Nonetheless, I would like to acknowledge the support and help of those who contributed the production of these performances: Miriam Basilio, Bik Van der Pol, Ilana Boltvinik, Andrea Ferreyra, RoseLee Goldberg, Erin Donnelly, Rosanna Flouty, Enrique Guerrero, Summer Guthery, Laurence Kardish, Anthony Kiendl, Michelle Marxuach, Catherine McDermott, Maria Jose Montalva, Anthony Huberman, Amy Owen, Allison Peters, Sara Reisman, Guillermo Santamarina, Itala Schmelz, Dannielle Tegeder, Encarnación Teruel, Chuck Thurow, Stefanie Wenner, and Wendy Woon—all of them, at different times, were receptive and trusting of the seeds of ideas for these works and became instrumental in their realization. I owe deep thanks to Jorge Pinto, who enthusiastically supported the creation of this anthology, to Rebecca Roberts, who edited these texts with superb precision, to my wife, Dannielle Tegeder, who encourages me and has patiently endured all of these performances, to Jeff Eaton, whose research and organizational support is simply invaluable to me, and to Tomas Hernández-Pumarejo, who allowed me to quote him extensively and inspired the text that gives the title to this book. Finally, I am permanently grateful to Ryan Hill, indefatigable performer, artist, educator, friend, and collaborator, who joined me in many of these projects and continues to let me subject him to my hybrid performative forays. The greatest joy of performing, to me, is not only to be able to connect with the public, but with friends and collaborators who can partake in the uncertainty, complicity, and joyful discovery that comes along with sharing a stage—or a lectern.

Theatrum Anatomicum
(Or, How to Dissect a Melodrama)
(2002)

For Tomás López-Pumarejo

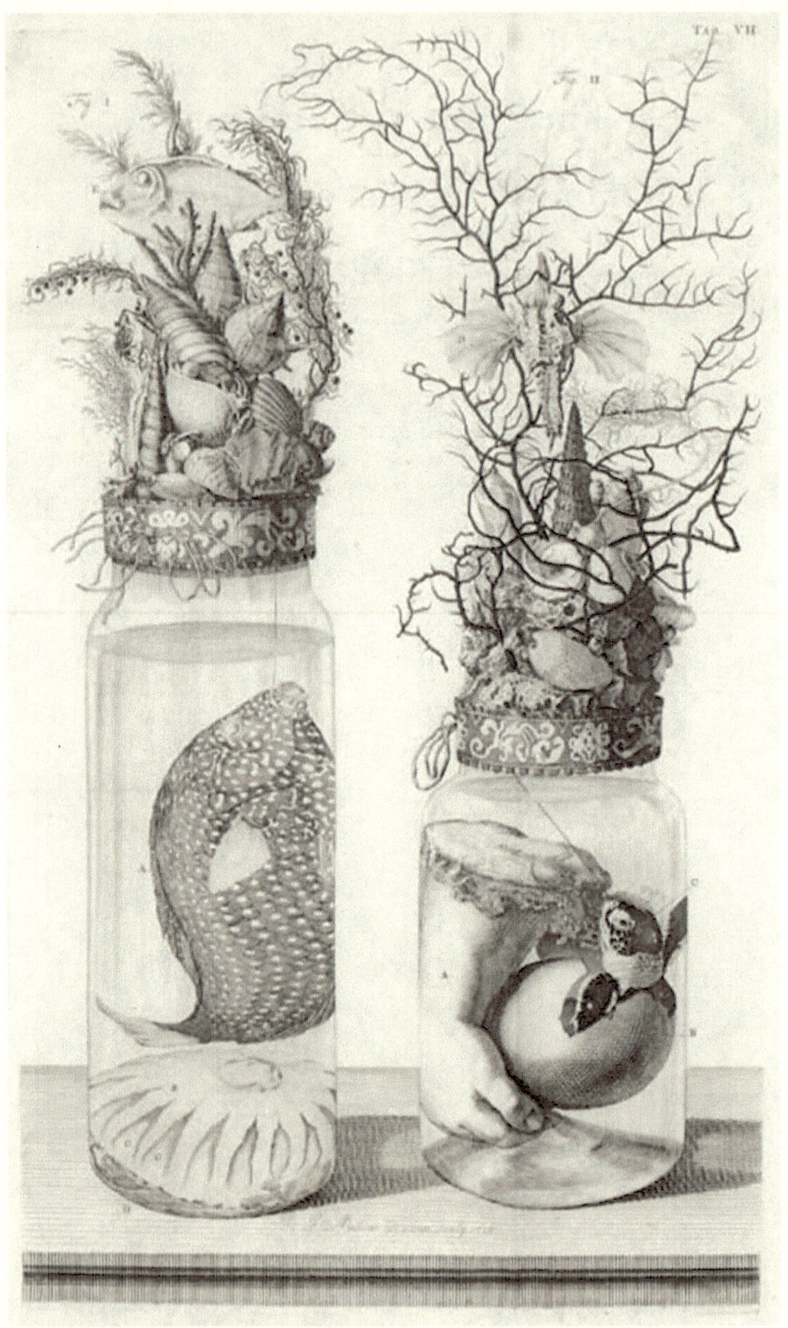

Theatrum Anatomicum (Or, How to Dissect a Melodrama) was first performed in summer 2002 at P.S.1 Contemporary Art Center in Long Island City, New York, by Pablo Helguera and Ryan Hill. The performance was part of the artists' multidisciplinary project Instituto de la Telenovela (Soap Opera Institute), a traveling research organization that examines the sociocultural impact of Latin American soap operas, or telenovelas, around the world. The performance was also presented at IFA-Gallery Bonn (2002), the Old Anatomical Theatre, London (2004), and Basis voor actuele kunst (BAK), Utrecht (2004). It consists of two synchronized lectures delivered simultaneously on dissimilar subjects: the origin and development of the soap opera genre in Latin America and the theatrical dimension of anatomical demonstrations in the Netherlands in the seventeenth century.

Appearing
Pablo Helguera, lecturer
Ryan Hill, lecturer

The performance space is arranged like a theater in the round; the audience surrounds the two speakers, who lecture and show slides simultaneously, aided by two slide projectors, two screens, and two speakers.

Pablo Helguera
Ladies and gentlemen, welcome to this evening's presentation. We believe that through this practical demonstration you will come to grasp the important aspects of the form of communication that is our subject tonight as well as its effects on society in general.

Ryan Hill
Peter the Great had one of the most spectacular collections of objects of wonder, including both *naturalia* and *artificialia*—what we know as a *Wunderkammern*, or cabinet of curiosities. Within it are works by Friedrick Ruysch, a Dutch anatomist, botanist, and embalmer who deserves a closer look. Ruysch, through various innovative methods, made a number of seemingly (to our eyes)

feng shui–inspired arrangements of dead bodies for moral, didactic, scientific, and artistic purposes. Many of them are on view today in St. Petersburg, where the czar's collection is held. When you look at these images you may wonder how such a fascination with the artistic representation of death arose.

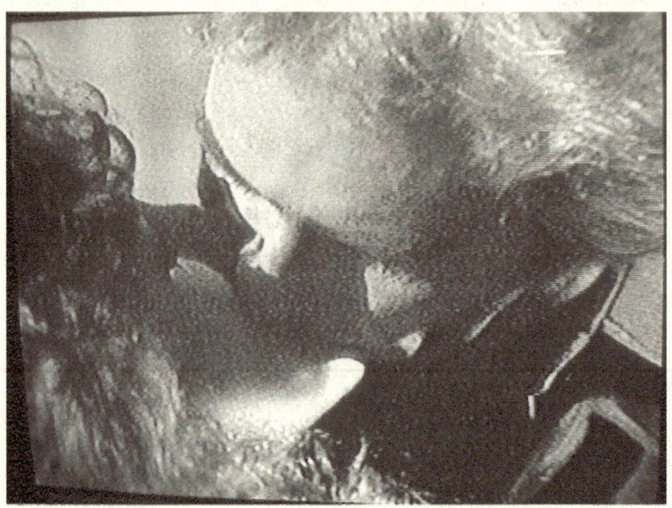

Helguera

At the end of the summer of 1992, after the fall of Communism, the Russian Commonwealth television channel Ostankino began broadcasting the 1970s Mexican series *Los Ricos también lloran* ("The rich also cry," or, in Russian, *Bogaty tozhe plachut*). *Los Ricos* is an old, low-budget, and melodramatic telenovela. The main story is that of a mother in search of her lost child. The public response to the thirteen-year-old soap opera was immediate and powerful, and it is estimated that 70 percent of the Russian population—approximately 200 million people—regularly tuned in, making it one of the most watched television series in history. Its final broadcast generated nation-wide mourning. Verónica Castro, who played the protagonist, was almost grandmotherly at the time the show became popular in Russia. When she traveled to that country she was—to her surprise—met by ecstatic crowds and adoring fans, many of whom, both men and women, cried uncontrollably when they got close to her. She was personally received by Boris Yeltsin at the Kremlin. In July 1998 *Los Ricos* was still being broadcast in Bosnia and Croatia, providing one of the few things that brought Serbians and Croatians together.

These few facts demonstrate the international impact of telenovelas:

- A few years ago, some mosques in Abidjan, Ivory Coast, decided to bring forward prayer time during Ramadan. This gesture saved thousands of the faithful from a painful dilemma—whether to do their religious duty or watch the latest episode of *Amor en silencio*, a Mexican television melodrama that has turned the whole country into telenovela addicts.
- At one time Fidel Castro scheduled staff meetings around the same telenovela, which was watched in Cuba by a record 85 percent of the total potential audience.
- In Cáceres, a small town in the province of Andalucía, Spain, there is a monument to María, the protagonist of the telenovela *Simplemente María* ("Simply Maria"), paid for by fans.
- In China the Brazilian telenovela *A Escrava Isaura* ("Slave girl Isaura") had an audience of 450 million in 1985. Twenty-eight million watched in Poland in 1986.
- A significant number of babies appear to have been named after telenovela characters. This practice, which once only belonged to Latin America, is now common in countries like Poland, the Philippines, and Ghana. In the national registries of these countries, names such as Marimar, María Mercedes, and Gabriel and Gabriela appear after the release dates of soap operas featuring those characters.
- Sales of blond hair dye have gone up in countries where a main telenovela actress is blond.
- The 1997 Mexican telenovela *Esmeralda*, about a young blind woman, proved so moving that in Hungary a group of people started a fund to help her get her sight back.
- Today telenovelas earn billions of dollars a year worldwide, surpassing the annual earnings of the British Broadcasting Corporation's international programming.

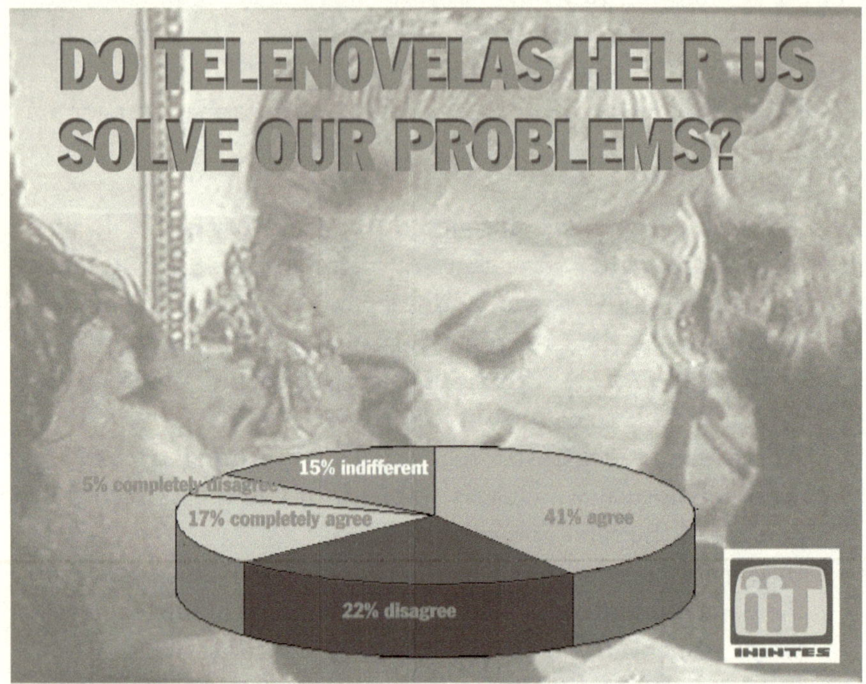

Whatever one thinks of the quality of telenovelas, they are undeniably effective products for reaching a wide public. The soap opera is the most effective broadcast advertising vehicle ever devised. It is also the most popular genre of television drama in the world today and probably in the history of television: no other form of televised fiction has attracted more viewers in more countries over a longer period of time.

But now let us discuss how the phenomenon of the telenovela originated. We will also examine how this dramatic genre has been underestimated and how it should be regarded as an art and, even further, a science.

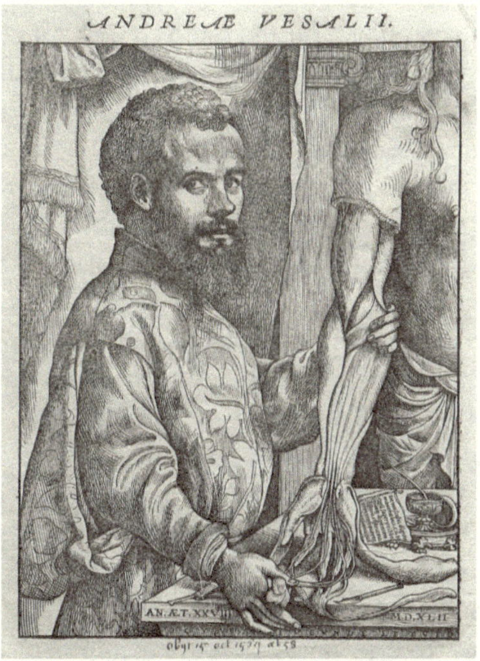

Hill

To answer these questions we need to go back to 1543. That year this man, Andreas Vesalius, gave birth to the modern science of anatomy through the publication of *De Humani Corporis Fabrica* ("Of the fabric of the human body"). This book, which was published when Vesalius was teaching anatomy and dissection at the University of Padua, is a milestone in the history of medicine and of Western civilization.

The work is believed to have been illustrated by Titian's atelier, and it marks the beginning of an era in which anatomical technique became an art form in and of itself, a topic we will examine here. Vesalius's work became widely popular in Europe in a very short time, and the scientific practice of anatomy proliferated.

Helguera

In 1930 the manager of a Chicago radio station approached a detergent company with a proposal for a daily fifteen-minute serialized radio drama. The program featured an Irish-American widow and her young, unmarried daughter—the first soap opera. The term "soap opera" was born precisely because it referred to the original advertiser and to the excessive dramatism, similar to that of the operatic genre, with which the domestic story was told.

By 1937 soap operas dominated the daytime commercial radio schedule and had become a crucial network programming strategy. The genre attracted such major sponsors as Procter & Gamble, Pillsbury, and General Foods, some of which still sponsor soap operas today. Most network soap operas were produced by advertising agencies, and some were even owned by the sponsoring client. In some cases during World War II, the advertising continued even when the sponsor's products were not available for sale, as story and product were practically inseparable.

Soap operas were something that members of a community could experience, talk about, and enjoy together.

Hill

After the death of Vesalius and the political and economic changes in Europe in the late-sixteenth century, northern Europe took up the development of anatomy. The study of anatomy was founded on the principles of dissection, and this practice, both an art and a science, served dual purposes of education and spectacle. This ambivalence of purpose created interesting moral issues, which we shall explore.

We go to Leiden, in 1590. The united provinces of the Netherlands had proclaimed independence in 1581, and throughout the sixteenth century the Dutch constantly challenged English authority over world trade. The seventeenth century would be their golden age, a time of commercial prosperity, colonial expansion, religious tolerance, and cultural achievement.

The science of anatomy also went through a golden period, flourishing in the Netherlands at the University of Leiden, founded in 1575 by William of Orange and modeled on the Academy of Geneva, an important center of Calvinistic teaching. By the early seventeenth century Leiden had an international reputation as a center of theology, science, and medicine.

The university attracted some of the most brilliant scientific minds of the time. Hermann Boerhaave and Nicolaes Tulp, who were largely responsible for Leiden's reputation in the study of medicine, spent their professional lives there. Boerhaave's status as one of the greatest physicians of that era lies partly in his attempts to collect, arrange, and systematize the mass of medical information that had accumulated up to that time.

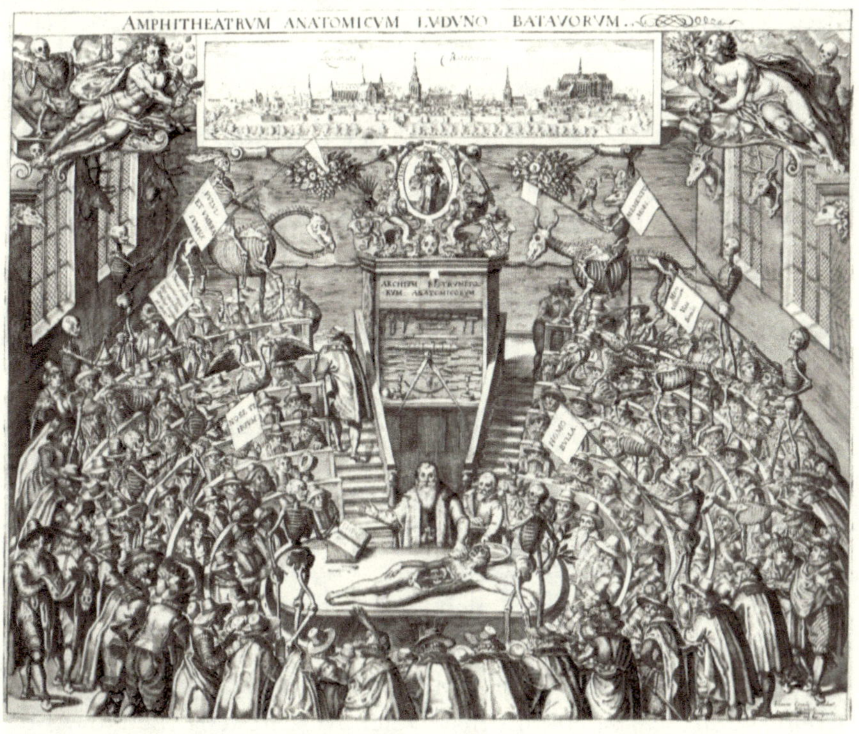

The systematization of the teaching of human anatomy along with the development and refinement of the anatomist's skills resulted in the evolution of the science from merely educational to fully spectacular. Around 1590 the Theatrum Anatomicum in Leiden, an anatomical theater, hosted special lectures during the winter months by the famous Dr. Pieter Pauw—public dissections of the bodies of freshly executed criminals. These dissections were eagerly anticipated events in the calendar of Leiden's spectacles. All the most important people of the town attended: senators and rectors of the university and burgomasters and aldermen along with medical students and faculty. The back benches were filled by the paying public. There were music, food and drink, and gossip; the smell of incense partially covered the smell of the putrefying corpses. The Theatrum was one of the great spectacles in town, with a public following like that of a concert or film today.

Helguera

In 1958 the first telenovela was aired. The commercial model was taken from American soap operas, but the scriptwriters borrowed stories from Cuban radio melodramas that had been successful at the cigar factories. The first melodrama was *El Derecho de nacer* ("The right to be born"), about a black woman who gives birth to a white son. It had racial and class tensions and undertones and was also a story of love, quintessential soap opera elements that made it extremely popular.

In the early years the Mexican television company Televisa experimented with a variety of telenovela formulas, but it soon became clear that the masses favored modern-day Cinderella narratives, fairy tales of social ascendance. This was a comfortable way for viewers to escape from their labor, offering hope, distraction, and, ultimately, a happy ending.

The perfect example of this formula is the Peruvian soap *Simplemente María,* the ultimate telenovela. It tells the story of María, a maid who goes to night school and becomes a fashion designer. After its debut in Peru in 1969, registration in evening literacy courses skyrocketed, as did sales of Singer sewing machines.

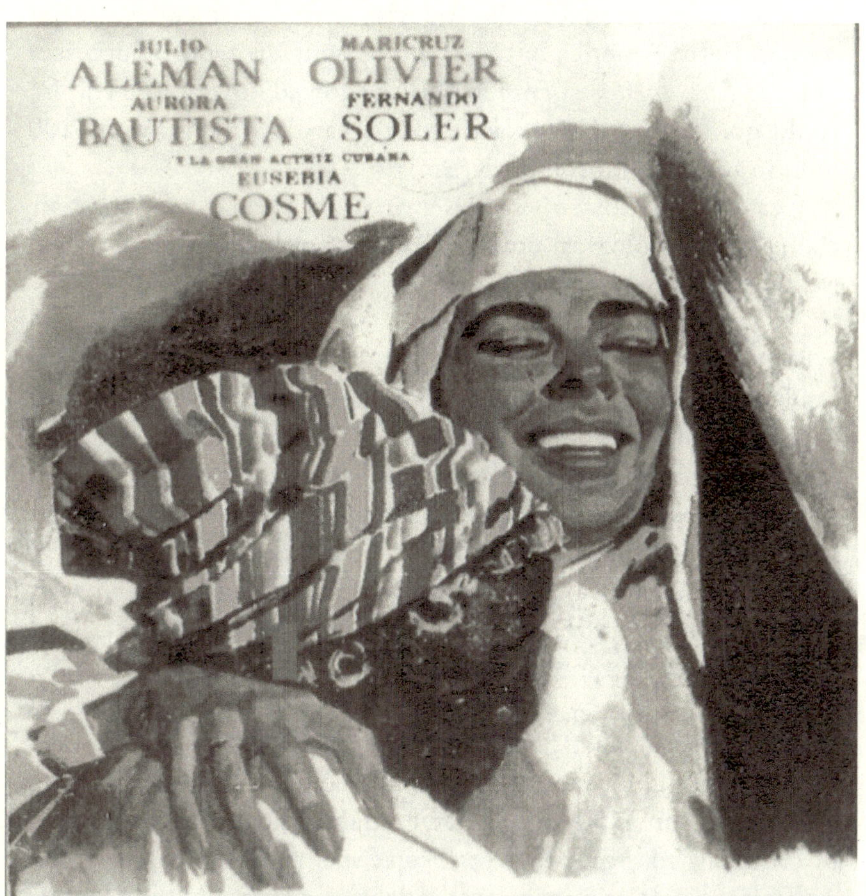
JULIO
ALEMAN
MARICRUZ
OLIVIER
AURORA
BAUTISTA
FERNANDO
SOLER
EUSEBIA
COSME
EL DERECHO
DE NACER
DE LA OBRA DRAMATICA DE FELIX B. CAIGNET
TITO DAVISON

Soon telenovela producers like Televisa started seeing sales rise not only in Latin America but also throughout the world. Successes like *Los Ricos también lloran* in Russia showed how far the empire could go. During the 1990s Televisa's earnings grew from $100 million to nearly $1 billion a year.

Certainly the soap opera was a very successful invention financially; its psychological power, also, was not lost on the powerful media moguls who produced them.

Hill

Leiden's Theatrum Anatomicum became a sort of *Wunderkammern*. Visitors could see a variety of tableaux made of rearticulated human and animal skeletons, including those of ferrets, horses, sheep, and goats. In most cases the human skeletons had belonged to criminals; a cattle thief's skeleton might be perched on top of that of an ox. The skeletons held pennants with moralizing *memento mori*, reminding audience members that they, too, would one day die. A book of the period mentions that visitors to the anatomy theater in Leiden could view an elephant's head and a whole variety of death-related artifacts, such as Egyptian mummies and Roman burial items. The centerpiece was a Tree of Knowledge with an Eve offering an apple to a skeletal Adam. The use of the corpses of criminals to create these tableaux was regarded as moral, because, it was felt, criminals owed a debt to society and the tableaux themselves were edifying.

Helguera

We have selected the 1997 Mexican version of the telenovela *Esmeralda* as an example of how a telenovela works and what its components are.

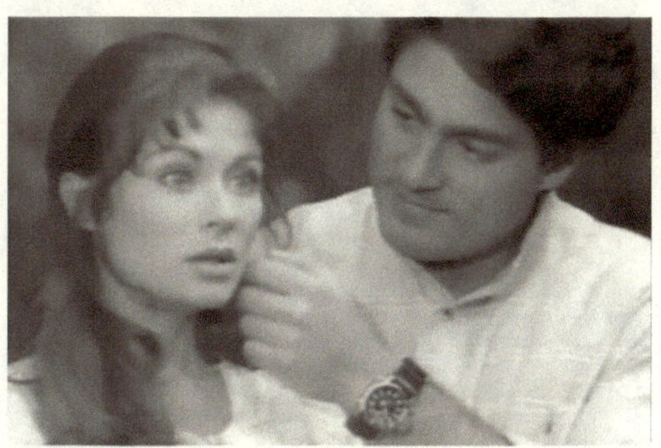

Esmeralda Peñarreal de Velasco is a poor, blind village girl, an orphan since birth. She is in love with José Armando, who also secretly loves her. In a fit of passion, José kisses Esmeralda. This creates with a conflict with his fiancée, Lucero, whom he is scheduled to marry in due time. Lucero, however, is in love with Adrian, a worker from the hacienda.

José's secret crush is soon discovered by his father, Don Rodolfo, who indignantly tries to banish Esmeralda from the town. He allies with Doctor Malaver, who loves Esmeralda and cannot bear to see her marry anyone else. The doctor had been deformed in the fire from which he saved Esmeralda as a child. He secretly knows that she can recover her sight, but he doesn't want her to see his ugly face.

In the climax of the story, Doña Fátima, José's mother, confesses that he is not her real son. It is discovered that a maid switched José and Esmeralda at birth. (It is never explained how the white hacienda owners never suspected the true origins of their decidedly Indian-looking son, while the white village girl with the beautiful green eyes roamed around the house.) All this leads to a happy ending, of course, after 137 episodes of further complications.

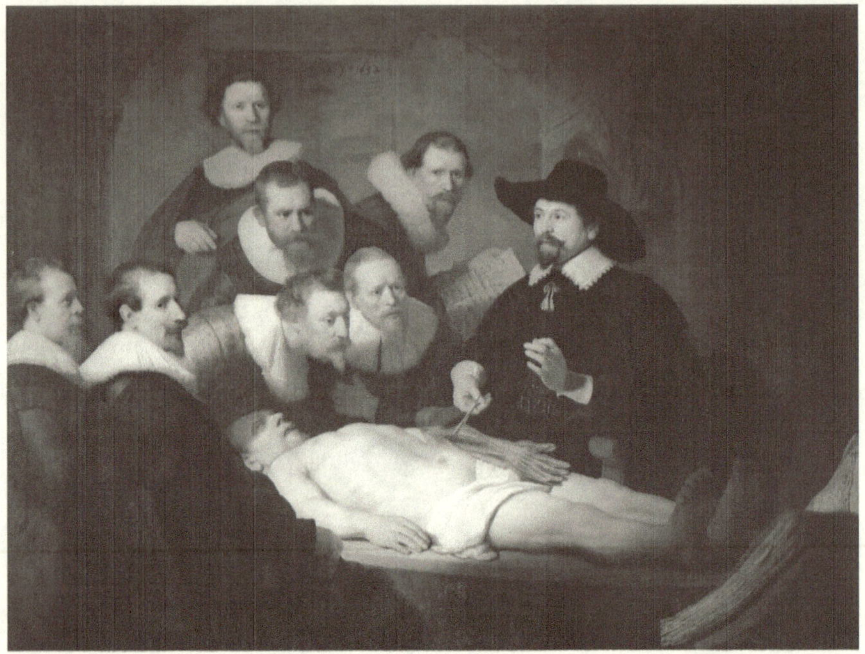

Hill

There is no better way to understand the spirit of the time than to look at this painting by Rembrandt van Rijn at age twenty-six. Rembrandt, living in Leiden at the time, was interested in human anatomy. A biographer says that he kept four severed human limbs in his house, cut by Vesalius himself. The references to Vesalius's *De Humani Corporis Fabrica* in this painting are very clear.

Rembrandt makes a very clear division between the death of the corpse and the vitality of the doctors; the painting is a powerful representation of the contrast between life and death. It is also a homage to the dexterity of the anatomist: instead of showing guts and blood, the artist has presented Tulp working on a perfectly clean corpse, explaining the parts and movements of the muscles of the hand.

Helguera

The telenovela developed from literary forms rooted in Romanticism and those with serial components, such as the nineteenth-century French and English novels that appeared chapter by chapter in newspapers.

According to scholar Tomás López-Pumarejo, the defining quality of the soap opera is its seriality: it appears in a series of individual installments. The viewer's understanding of the story depends on knowledge of what has happened in previous episodes, and each episode always leaves a loose end for the next episode to take up. Serial characters change across episodes (they age and even die), and they have histories and memories.

López-Pumarejo divides soap operas into two basic narrative types: "open" soap operas, in which there is no end point toward which the action of the narrative moves (this includes all United States daytime serials—*General Hospital* and *All My Children*, for example—and the wave of primetime American soaps in the 1980s, such as *Dallas* and *Dynasty*); and "closed" soap operas, in which the narrative, no matter how long, does eventually close. The closed format is more common in Latin America. Telenovelas may stretch over three or four months and hundreds of episodes, but they are designed to end.

Hill

Incidentally, it is at this time that the vanitas as a subject for painting first emerged, in Holland. Various paintings treating the ephemeral nature of life were made, in a tradition that endured well into the nineteenth century. Painters such as Jacob van Ruisdael depicted landscapes with elements such as cemeteries and other symbols of the ephemeral nature of life and the inescapability of death.

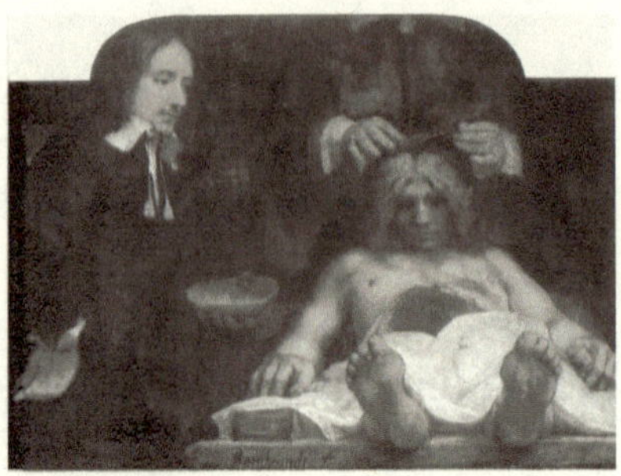

Rembrandt painted this work twenty-five years after *The Anatomy Lesson of Dr. Tulp*, at a mature stage of his life, and it is much cruder than the earlier work. It is safe to say that his outlook on life had changed, becoming bleaker.

Helguera

According to Pumarejo, telenovelas revolve around the tension between the needs and desires of heterosexual and monogamic couples and the world of social conventions. In telenovelas the tension between these two apparently opposed imperatives leads eventually to their reconciliation. The constant clash of tradition against modernity keeps the dramatic energy going.

Quoting Pumarejo again, these are some of the features that characterize the telenovela:

- Telenovelas are stories of love, primarily rooted in the Romantic novel. Scholar Assumpta Roura calls them "pornography for women" because of their visual focus on (nongenital) passion.
- Telenovelas are based around dramas of identity, a staple of melodrama, such as: "Who is my father or mother?" "Where is my daughter or son?"
- Contrary to "male" narratives, domestic or "female" fiction like telenovelas deals more with consequences than action and more with the family circle than with the public world. As in Ibsen's and Chekhov's naturalist dramas, in telenovelas characters experience the public world in the domestic sphere. Most of the action takes place in interior settings, and narrative progress relies on close-up views and conversation.

Hill

The fashion of depicting anatomical scenes through art and using anatomical imagery as a metaphor for life and death reached its climax in the work of a scientist and artist who is in many ways the originator of the modern museum by way of the cabinet of curiosities. This man is Friedrick Ruysch, professor of anatomy in Leiden and Amsterdam, notable for his methods of embalming and preserving bodies.

Ruysch gave the first descriptions of bronchial blood vessels and the vascular networks of the heart and made a great number of other important discoveries in anatomy. However, it is his injection method that allowed him to create the assemblages that we know him for, 1,300 of which Peter the Great acquired and brought to St. Petersburg. Some of Ruysch's assemblages are very straightforward: for example, a prostitute's skull kicked by the leg bones of a baby. He used his knowledge of preserving flesh (in alcohol and other formulas) to make arrangements of dead infants in glass jars. His most popular assemblages, now lost, were *vanitas mundi* tableaux, carefully placed arrangements of baby skeletons, kidney stones (commonly exhibited at the time), and flowers. Ruysch made about a dozen tableaux, also lost, with human skeletons and fetuses on the topic of death and the transiency of life.

Helguera

Today telenovelas are the main instrument of public health and literacy campaigns by organizations such as the United Nations. Telenovelas also sometimes unintentionally influence social attitudes and practices, such as when, for example, a leading character has a specific disease: the appearance of a breast cancer patient in *Cristal* (Venezuela, 1985) was followed by a surge in breast examinations in Venezuela and Spain.

The following quote by a viewer interviewed in soap opera magazine illustrates the way in which audiences from different parts of the world identify themselves with telenovela characters:

What I like about Marimar is that she has the same problems as we do. She's poor like us. Her house was burned down. They mistreated her. They degraded her. She's almost Filipina.

—Ligaya Magbanua, waitress, Manila

By and large, however, telenovelas promote traditional values, and while most stories have happy endings, they generally remain uncontroversial and rarely provide any real social or political critique. This is why at times in their history telenovelas have functioned as "opiates of the masses," that is, effective escapist tools that distract audiences from serious national problems faced by Latin American countries. It is well known that in Mexico in the 1980s and early 1990s programming of telenovelas increased in times of national crisis—part of a quid pro quo alliance between Televisa and the PRI, then the ruling party of the Mexican government. Telenovelas provide an unconscious and cathartic way to collectively deal with current social, racial, or economic conflicts, but in a way that does not become threatening to those in power.

At a conference in Russia in the mid 1990s, Emilio Azcarraga, Sr., then the owner of Televisa, candidly declared that telenovelas are made for "a fucked up social class that will never cease to be fucked up." For years a small group of people has profited from selling dreams of triumph, justice, and beauty to members of a social class who, paradoxically, only reaffirm their position by consuming them. After completing the circle of consumerism and conversion to corporate values, they are left alone to deal with the psychological vacuum and the biases reinforced by the stories. But telenovelas can also be a primary education tool for a nation. As writer Carlos Monsivais once noted, Televisa has had more impact in the education of the Mexican public than the ministry of education.

So what is the role of ethics in the spectacle of the telenovela? Where is the line between education and entertainment, between entertainment and manipulation, between moralistic preaching and true learning?

Hill

Perhaps we may better understand the origins of this sensibility by returning to seventeenth-century Holland. Just around the time when anatomical theaters and skeleton tableaux were in vogue, a Jew of Portuguese origin arrived Holland. His name was Baruch Spinoza, and his most important work is *Ethics*, published posthumously in 1677. Spinoza's *Ethics* deals in three distinct areas: it begins with metaphysics, goes into the psychology of the passions and the will, and finally sets forth an ethic based on the preceding two subjects. Spinoza thought that emotions were to be distrusted, that we would arrive at virtue and the "intellectual love of god" through the mind, that our attempts to make a profit would be moral as long as they were earnest.

In *Ethics* Spinoza presents the following precepts:

Helguera

This brings us to a series of questions about televised culture and its impact on the lives of those who consume it. How is it that we do not hold telenovela producers accountable for the emotional dependence and conservative indoctrination they impose on society at large?

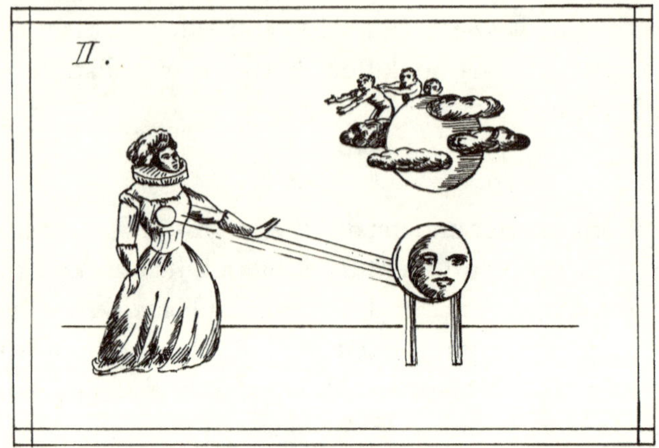

Hill

Precept II: *The body cannot determine the mind to thought, neither can the mind determine the body to motion nor rest, nor to anything else if there be anything else.*

In other words, the mind and the body are separate entities, at odds with each other, and emotions are their main disruptive force.

Helguera

We might think that it's OK to let ourselves go into a paradise of escapism in which our dreams are our own business. But what if those dreams prevent us from waking up?

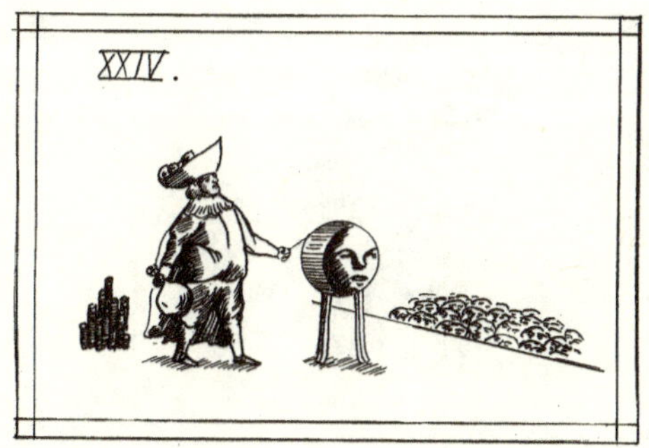

Hill

Precept XXIV: *To act absolutely in conformity with virtue, is, in us, nothing but acting, living, and preserving our being (these are things that have the same meaning) as reason directs, from the ground of seeking our own profit.*

In other words, Spinoza believed that the more each person strives for his own profit, the more virtue he possesses and thus the closer he gets to God. Spinoza's most famous principle is, "Each thing strives to persevere in its own being."

Helguera

And are we learning? Or have our emotions been seduced?

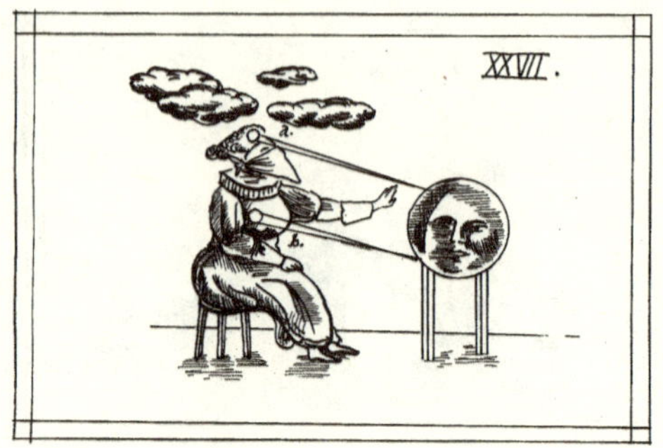

Hill
Precept XXVII: *We do not know that anything is certainly good or evil except that which actually leads to understanding, or which can prevent us from understanding.*

Helguera
And how do we determine that we really can perform with absolute freedom when someone else is the owner of our desires?

Hill
And last but not least—

Helguera
So should we sometimes let ourselves be ruled by our emotions?

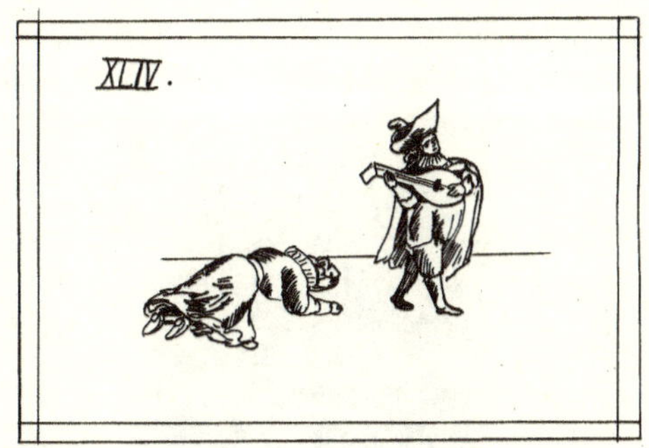

Hill
Precept XLIV: *Love and desire may be excessive.*

Helguera
Perhaps.

2003

PRIMER CONGRESO INTERNACIONAL DE PURIFICACION CULTURAL URBANA DE LA CIUDAD DE MEXICO

First Mexico City Congress of Urban Purification (2003)

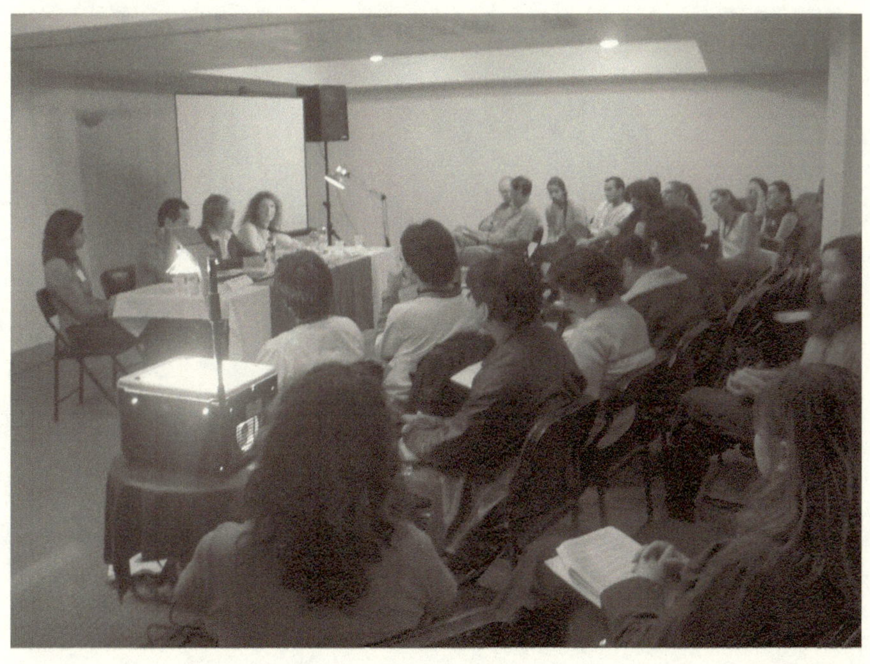

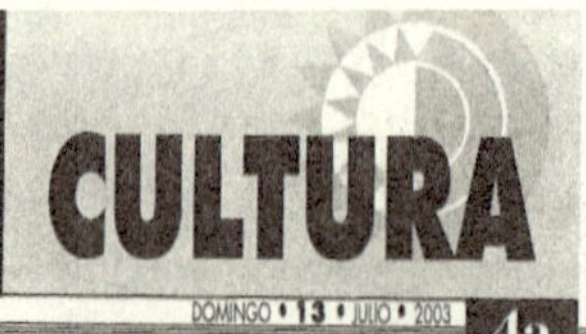

4a

ERICKA MONTAÑO GARFIAS

Sugieren en encuentro promover taller de sensibilización para políticos

Proponen artistas independientes remedios para *sanar* a la cultura

Asumen su responsabilidad en la desvinculación entre creadores e instituciones gubernamentales

Crear un consejo consultivo que vea a la cultura como una fuerza curativa, educar a los políticos en cuestiones culturales, dejar el arte en manos del Estado y de una comisión ultraconservadora, y desaparecer instituciones ligadas al arte y la cultura son las cuatro propuestas que se presentaron en el primer Congreso Internacional de Purificación Cultural Urbana de la Ciudad de México, organizado por creadores independientes, que se realizó este sábado y al que asistieron artistas, críticos de arte e investigadores.

Uno de los proyectos que se presentó en el congreso, en el que se denunció la falta de diálogo entre las autoridades y los artistas como una responsabilidad compartida, es la creación del consejo nacional para la curación de la cultura y las artes, promovido por artistas como Néstor Quiñones, Antonio Ortiz –*Gritón*–, Gabriel Macotela y Betania de la Vega, como informó ayer *La Jornada*.

El nuevo consejo parte de la idea "de que la cultura es una fuerza curativa"; tiene como objetivo, de acuerdo con su manifiesto de creación, "la defensa, promoción y difusión de todas aquellas expresiones culturales que propicien la evolución de la sociedad en su conjunto, estableciendo procesos de reflexión encaminados a elevar y

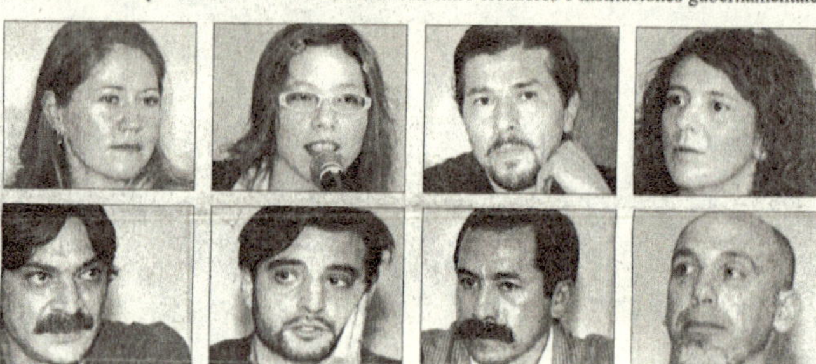

MARIA LUISA SEVERIANO

Martina Ridler, Ilana Boltvinik, Néstor Quiñones, Raquel Ontiveros, Marco Barrera Bassols, Pablo Helguera, Alberto Rivas Mercado y Ryan Hill, participantes en el primer Congreso Internacional de Purificación Cultural Urbana de la Ciudad de México

se manifestó por la desaparición ra en la ciudad es la falta de nistración de la cultura en los nicación en la difusión de la cul-

La Journada, cultural section, July 13, 2003

The Primer congreso de purificación cultural urbana de la ciudad de México *(First Mexico City Congress of Urban Purification) was a collaborative project by Ilana Boltvinik and Pablo Helguera made in response to the increasingly conservative climate of government-run cultural policy—or lack thereof—in Mexico. The project took the form of a conference in the Hotel de la Ciudad de Mexico in downtown Mexico City in May 2003. The project was not advertised as an artwork but as a real conference with a call for papers stating that "culture, like the environment, is polluted" and inviting submissions about to how to "purify" it. Many submissions were received, from as far away as Colombia, and six were selected for the conference. Six others were scripted and read by actors, unbeknownst to the audience. The six scripted submissions were in a sense responses to the six real submissions, formulating statements or points of view that are rarely expressed in academic or public forums.*

Following are two of the scripted papers read during the conference. "Elegy for the End of Institutional Time," read by Mexican curator Marco Barrera Bassols, who was playing himself, calls for the complete elimination of national arts funding—arguing that most funding ends up supporting the bureaucratic apparatus, not actual art making. At the time of the symposium, Rudolf Giuliani, former mayor of New York, had been hired by the Mexico City government as a security advisor. The series of proposed cultural measures read by performance artist Ryan Hill—playing an eponymous fictional character—who was introduced as director of a pro-Giuliani organization, proposed a U.S.-run cultural policy program for Mexico inspired by Giuliani's own conservative view of culture (not too long before, Giuliani, then mayor of New York City, had sought to take away funding from the Brooklyn Museum in response to its display of Chris Ofili's painting The Holy Virgin Mary*). This paper generated a small media scandal, fueled by outrage over the notion of U.S.-led cultural policy in Mexico, in the papers* La Jornada, Reforma, Universal, Milenio, *and others, which in turn led to a public debate on cultural policy, as originally hoped.*

Elegy for the End of Institutional Time

APPEARING

Marco Barrera Bassols, independent curator, Mexico City, playing himself

Marco Barrera Bassols

In 1941 the French composer Olivier Messiaen wrote *Quartet for the End of Times*, widely considered to be his masterpiece and without a doubt one of the most unique and aesthetically radical musical works of the twentieth century. But that's not all: Messiaen wrote the piece inside the German concentration camp of Görlitz, and it was performed there for the prisoners.

Messiaen's quartet has always been, in my view, the greatest example of the ability of art to transcend every kind of restriction, structure, institution, or yoke and affirm human nature in the face of political repression. Today repression is not as blatant as under the Third Reich, but we do live within repressive structures, smaller ones, built by the modern industrial aristocracy and imposed by an international economy run by corporations. To me Messiaen's work is a reminder that art is linked to freedom of expression, and it becomes ever more meaningful as a barometer of humanity under the rule of a repressive society.

However, art has another transformative function, which I regard as its higher mission: to dissolve the all-encompassing control of institutions and give us back our individuality. This is what I would like to speak about here, today.

Mexico's cultural projects, from the construction of its Metropolitan Cathedral to the Hotel de Mexico, have been characterized by their monumentality but also by the impossibility of their consummation, a result of our innate tendency toward baroque institutionalism, whether political, economic, social, or religious. In political terms, this tendency was perfectly expressed, as we all know, with the creation of the supreme epitome of this paradox: the Institutional Revolutionary Party.

Mexico's true problem is that despite PRI's loss of the presidency*—even if it is temporary—all of us Mexicans continue to behave instinctively as institutional revolutionaries. Our modernity as a society, which was so grandiosely proclaimed at midcentury by technocrats such as Miguel Alemán, has been only halfway attained. We did take part in the twentieth century, but only as obedient subjects who accepted the existing political and social structures, tolerated abuses, and implicitly supported the preservation of an anti-democratic system, full of injustice and contradiction. It is a natural result, given that we Mexicans are used to accepting reality as it is and just playing along, simply because it is more difficult to move against the current.

But artists and all of those who work in the cultural field are required to defy, question, and dissolve the status quo. Why do we have to accept government institutions telling us what is artistically valuable and what isn't? Why do we accept that a law student whose experience lies only in knowing where to move in a world of opaque alliances and corruption is suddenly given the power to decide what art is, what defines the deepest dimensions of human sensibility? What are institutions good for, and how can we be sure that they do not exist for their own benefit? How can we be sure that any academic format presented to us provides us with the truth of things? Why not suppose, for instance, that this symposium is not a discussion of ideas but rather a piece of theater in which all the presenters are actors? Or that everything we know is the result of a subliminal indoctrination practiced ever since our childhood, as alpha, beta, and gamma babies are brainwashed in the hospital nurseries of Aldous Huxley's *Brave New World*?

It is not my intention to be a solipsistic critic of reality, nor do I want to go back to the remote times of Greek skepticism. Nonetheless, it would be hard for anyone here today not to recognize that the current state of affairs in Mexico has turned all Mexicans, at base, into skeptics. No one among us believes in anything, everything is possible and everything is suspicious at the same time: in the end, our certainties are few. Reality, for us, has become frustratingly inaccessible, and it has become little more

* In 2000, the PRI, long the ruling party of Mexico, lost the election for the first time in seventy years to an opposition candidate.

than a world of references we sometimes accept and sometimes reject. We feel distanced from it precisely because of the institutional structures that have been imposed on us.

The antidote to all this, the liberating force, is art. Art is the most intimate human expression there is, the one that is hardest to control or govern and, as a result, the greatest weapon we have to break the useless structures that control our society.

Art doesn't require institutions. Art doesn't need culture councils or museums or artistic impresarios or specialists or critics, nor cultural supplements, galleries, or festivals. Any structure elaborated by the art world over the course of the twentieth century is part of what theorists have defined as the economy of culture. And as such, as in Plato's cave, it is a system of shadows that simulates the processes of art, but which in reality only uses those projections to justify a series of goals that have nothing to do with the production of art.

It goes without saying that in contemporary society overall, the economy of culture is fueled by galleries and jet-set collectors, but in Mexico it is primarily run by the government. So in our case art is more of a political and doctrinary tool than a financial one. Which is even more serious, because while art at the service of economy is a mere product, art at the service of political interests is propaganda and demagogy.

If we really seek to extricate ourselves from the labyrinth of doubts posed by our reality, if we truly want to experience art again, it is of utmost importance that we decentralize culture and dismantle the systems that run it. Funds that are directed to useless bureaucracies should instead be directed to artists with professional careers. Some may ask, who will organize the exhibitions, who will do the paperwork, who will promote, preserve, and collect? The answer: How many organizers do we have today who are truly effective and beneficial? How many masterworks have been created over the last years thanks to the Mexican government? How many more retrospectives by Juan Soriano and how many more government buildings by Abraham Zabludovsky do we have to endure in order to understand that the current structures are not good for us? Finally, in terms of collecting, it is a fact that Mexican museums have not had budgets for contemporary art since 1974, so lack of funding would not have any impact in this area anyway.

Messiaen didn't need a national council of culture in order to write his quartet in the Görlitz concentration camp; he only needed the yellowish soup the Nazis served him once a day. Picasso didn't ask for a grant to paint *Guernica*, Sor Juana didn't get a tenured university position and live in Las Lomas* nor did José Gorostiza write the most important Mexican poem of the twentieth century—*Muerte sin fin* (Death without end)—on a life-long grant from CONACULTA†. He did it, paradoxically, out of a bureaucratic office after working hours, and as an escape from the pressures of his life. In other words, the great structures do not guarantee great art but may even block it. And if Mexican art is considered central to the history of modernity, it is not thanks to the PRI but to those Mexicans who have known how to express themselves through the eloquence of artistic language.

The medieval mystic Angelus Silesius wrote, "The rose blooms because it blooms, without why." And Saint Bernard wrote, "Love finds its own reward in itself." Paraphrasing these thinkers, I say art blooms because it blooms, without why, and it finds its reward in its own expression. Everything else is external: commercialization, promotion, social hierarchy, benefits for other enterprises and uses. The natural and disinterested growth of art makes it independent of any artificial structure created by human imagination. Art can escape those structures, which create a world in which few benefit and all are losers in the long run.

In Mexico we have been too happy to have transitioned from "noble savages" to "good institutional revolutionaries."‡ It is time to become critical, independent thinkers. For that, it is necessary to reclaim art for ourselves. In this city of kidnappings, the greatest and least discussed of them all is the kidnapping of art and culture by our government. Let's take it back from those institutions, and once we do we shall see the new Mexican century open before us in all its splendor.

---

* A well-off residential neighborhood in Mexico City.

† *Consejo nacional para la cultura y las artes* (Mexico's national council of the arts)

‡ This is a reference to a famous book by Venezuelan journalist Carlos Rangel: *Del Buen salvaje al buen revolucionario* (1976). Published in English as *The Latin Americans*

Urban Purification Proposal

APPEARING
Performance artist **Ryan Hill**, playing Ryan Hill, Assistant Director, Department of Cultural Services of the Rudolph Giuliani Commission of Mexico City

Ryan Hill
Thank you for coming. As assistant director of the Department of Cultural Services and assigned representative of the Rudolph Giuliani Commission for this congress, I would like to start my presentation by speaking about our projects related to the improvement of the cultural life of Mexico City. After that I will get into the specifics of our cultural program, known as PROLICU.

As you may or may not know, the Commission is an independent, not-for-profit philanthropic organization that focuses its energies on solving the current problems in Mexico City where culture is concerned. The Department of Cultural Services—created in early 2002 to increase the Commission's range of activity—has as its mission to condemn and abolish each and every abuse of life and humanity and bring to light and cleanse all cultural practices that are hazardous to mental health.

From its very beginnings, the Commission has made an uninterrupted stand against brutal treatment, criminal practices, and abuse in relation to social and cultural human hygiene, following as its main principle the emphasis on moral renovation Rudolf W. Giuliani introduced as mayor of the City of New York between 1994 and 2001. The Commission has become a really effective force in the promotion of changes in this area.

Our Program of Cultural Cleanup, or *Programa de limpieza cultural*, known as PROLICU, is dedicated to the research and identification of any violation of cultural hygiene, in both the psychiatric and physical senses. Although the Commission is a relatively young organization, it has already made an in-depth cultural study with the help of national and international experts in order to present, in the most complete way possible, our action plan for the cultural cleansing of this city.

I will now describe the first stages of PROLICU.

Program of Cultural Purification (PROLICU)

In 2002 the Commission launched this international program for the cultural purification of Mexico City. The project, carefully developed with the objective of completely reforming the life of Mexico City through a thorough cultural cleanup, consists of a series of key steps that are yet to be implemented.

Phase 1: Case Study and Cultural Evaluation

The general PROLICU committee, composed of members of the government who are knowledgeable in the field of the arts, will carefully analyze the cultural program of each one of the city's museums, houses of culture, universities, schools, galleries, and activity centers open to the public, identifying immoral activities where they occur—not necessarily in every institution, although it is estimated that 78 percent of cultural centers in Mexico City host such activities to some extent and are therefore in need of profound renovation.

Phase 2: Cleanup and Renovation

All directors, curators, museum administrators, and employees of government-run galleries, cultural centers, and community centers whose cultural activities present a challenge to authority will be immediately dismissed without notice.

Phase 3: Reprogramming, Regulation, and Quotas

After the selection of new directors to fill the vacancies created by Phase 2, a new organization will be announced: the Commission of Morality and Public Decency (also known as *Comisión de moralidad y decencia pública*, or COMODEPU, a principal organ of PROLICU, which will supervise all cultural entities in Mexico City, public and private, and grant approval of artistic projects on the basis of civic decency. Every exhibition project, concert, publication, or expression designed to be transmitted to a public larger than eight people will be presented to the authorities of COMODEPU and in order to receive approval must do the following:

- promote a positive image of Mexico City
- completely lack reference to sexual acts or attack sexual morality
- refrain from the use of obscene words
- not invoke the name of God or Mexico in vain nor profanely under any circumstance
- use no foreign words other than English (local indigenous languages excepted) unless to announce commercial products

Those cultural producers and/or administrators who participate in works supposedly of an artistic nature that do not follow these rules will be immediately subject to fines and quotas of up to US $10,000. Additionally, any work that is considered to make, either directly or metaphorically, any slanderous attack of a political, social, religious, or economic nature will be confiscated and examined by COMODEPU and deemed appropriate or inappropriate for public viewing. Exempted from this rule are artists and creators who have received lifelong scholarships from CONACULTA.

Phase 4: Education and Progress

Simultaneously to Phase 3, the Commission will establish a program of revision of the artistic curriculum in Mexico City schools, in collaboration with the Ministry of Education. In this program, designed by experts, deficiencies in the current educational system will be addressed and special classes will be provided for the training of future artists.

Phase 5: Unforeseen Changes

The Commission will replace any director of a cultural institution whenever it deems it necessary without making any explanation of his or her dismissal. Possible reasons for such dismissals include the following:

1. expressing aesthetic points of view that differ from the preestablished guidelines for the artistic advancement of the city
2. unannounced activities
3. collaborations with international institutions that are not sanctioned by the government

Phase 6: Social Function of Museums and Other Cultural Institutions

The Commission will establish a special calendar detailing the availability of all cultural centers, whether public or private, for programming. Under the instructions of CONACULTA, these spaces will make themselves available to realize the following, in strict order of priority:

1. government-related and official events
2. official exhibitions and events organized by CONACULTA
3. exhibitions, lectures, and events by government-approved artists

These few phases in the first plan to accomplish a true renovation of the management of culture in Mexico City will no doubt immediately benefit all those who appreciate art in the city and will also provide a more efficient mechanism for the development of the city's cultural program.

Parallel Lives

(2003)

CARNEGIE HALL PROGRAM

SEASON 1944-1945

FIRE NOTICE — Look around *now* and choose the nearest exit to your seat. In case of fire walk (not run) to *that* Exit. Do not try to beat your neighbor to the street.

PATRICK WALSH, *Fire Commissioner.*

Wednesday Evening, October 25th, at 8:30 o'clock

Florence Foster Jenkins

Coloratura Soprano

Assisted by

The PASCARELLA CHAMBER MUSIC SOCIETY

COSME McMOON, *Pianist*

•

Programme

I.

ENGLISH SONGS

Phyllis .... *Young*
Love Has Eyes .... *Bishop*
Lo, Here the Gentle Lark .... *Bishop*
(Flute obbligato by Oreste De Sevo)
MME. JENKINS

II.

Quartet, Allegro con brio, Op. 54, No. 19 .... *Haydn*
PASCARELLA CHAMBER MUSIC SOCIETY

Program Continued on Second Page Following

Parallel Lives was first performed on December 8, 2003, as part of The Museum of Modern Art's Mediascope program at the Gramercy Theater in New York.

Five phonographs recorded and replayed sections of the performance, which also included a PowerPoint presentation.

Appearing
Pablo Helguera, lecturer

Pablo Helguera

In New York City during the waning days of World War II, a peculiar event unfolded on Carnegie Hall's famous stage. Hundreds of people lined up at the box office for the last glorious performance of one of the most unique singers of any generation.

But this singer, a woman in her seventies, was considered by many to be the worst singer of all time. Critics claimed that she sounded like a drunken cuckoo, while others described her as "the first diva of the sliding scale." However, she had remained unfazed by these criticisms and plowed ahead through one of the most remarkable careers in the history of classical music. Her name was Florence Foster Jenkins.

Madame Jenkins had no sense of rhythm or intonation. Her voice vanished into thin air in the upper register, making listening both comical and unpleasant. On top of that, her repertoire included some of the most difficult opera arias in the classical canon. A favorite staple of her program was the Queen of the Night's aria in Mozart's *The Magic Flute.* Never in memory had a singer so untalented tried to climb to such ambitious heights and with such embarrassing results. And yet she had become a star. Even Enrico Caruso was said to be fond of her. There was something in her story that made her larger than life.

Florence Foster was born in 1868 in Wilkes-Barre, Pennsylvania, daughter of a banker. In her youth she expressed a desire to become a professional musician, but her father, set in his Victorian ways, did not approve of this profession and hoped instead that she would lead a domestic life. As a result, the ambitious Florence eloped with a doctor, Frank Thornton. Her marriage did not last, and she barely could support herself with piano lessons, but soon her father passed away and, having forgiven her, left her a vast sum of money. This was the true beginning of her operatic career.

Florence used her money wisely, financing small solo recitals and creating around herself a society of women to support her musical endeavors. She was herself a supporter of the musical arts and created a small fund to help young musicians. An expert organizer, she put together benefits and recitals and usually appeared in the lineup of performers. She was known for selling tickets to her recitals personally, one by one—a direct connection with the audience was extremely important to her. At the end of every concert she asked her public to write to her and tell her what songs they liked the most.

A recital by Florence Foster Jenkins was something without equal. For her, interpretation of the music was not enough; every performance included carefully arranged scenery and costumes.

One of her favorite characters was the "angel of inspiration," whose costume included a pair of giant white wings. For another favored number, the Spanish song *Clavelitos*, she wore a large shawl and carried a basket full of red carnations, which she threw into the audience to the cadence of the song. Once, at the end of this number, the ovation was such that she had an assistant pick up the flowers and repeated the singing and throwing all over again. Her loyal and eternal accompanist, Cosme McMoon, played her favorite Rachmaninoff and Mozart arias along with some less challenging songs of the period.

Madame Jenkins's theories of vocal perfection were hard to understand, but for her they were perfectly logical. Once, after she was hit by a taxicab in New York City, she sent a box of cigars to the offender with a note thanking him, because "since the accident" she could sing an octave higher. When she was recording, every first version was "perfect, beyond improvement," and on one occasion she claimed that she had heard the versions of the *Queen of the Night* aria from Mozart's *The Magic Flute* by the sopranos Tetrazzini and Hempel and that, without a doubt, hers was "the best of the three."

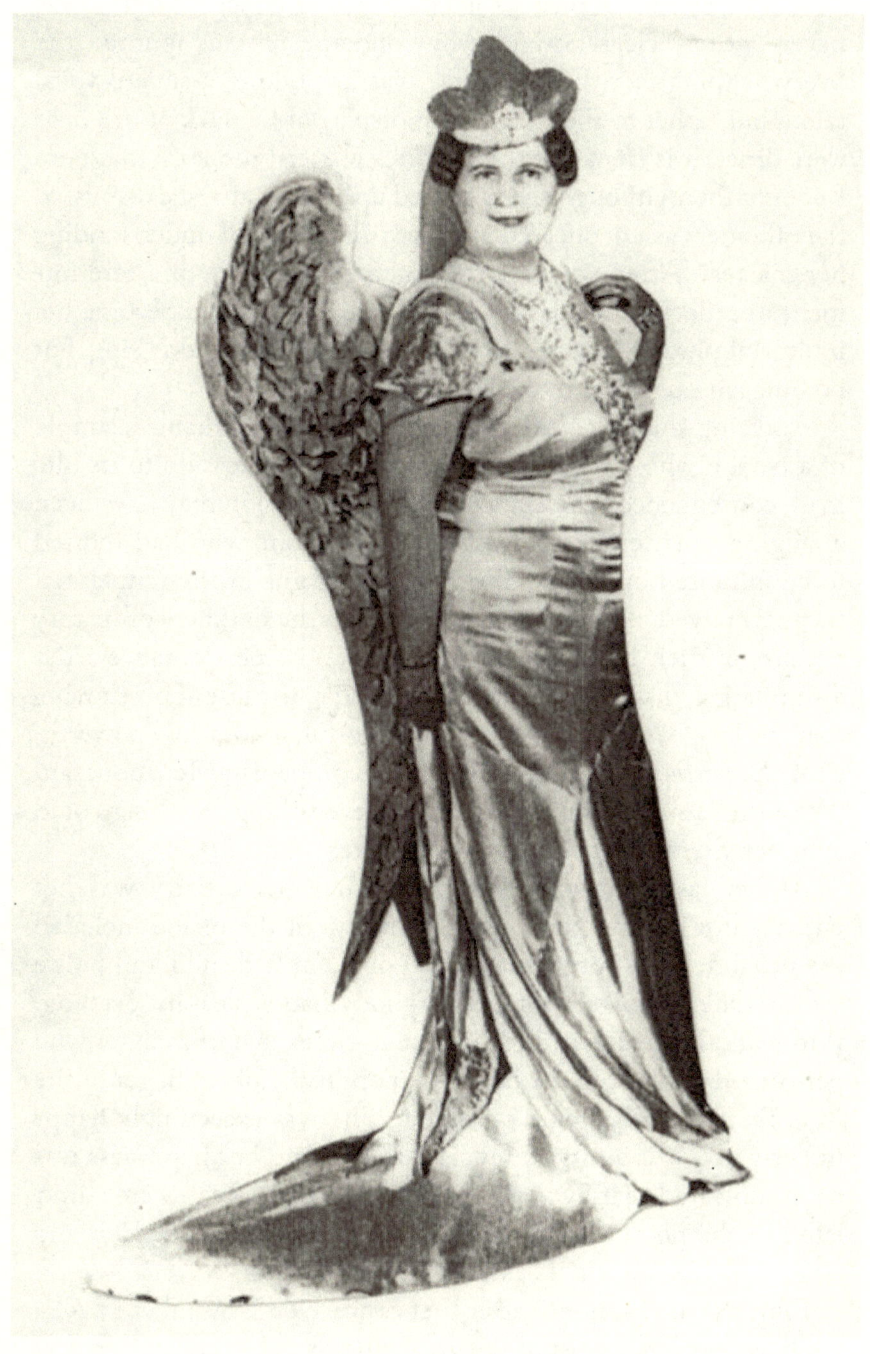

It is clear that audiences laughed at her concerts, but it was never entirely clear how or why Madame Jenkins ignored the overwhelming fact that her fame was not due to a superb vocal talent but rather to the flamboyant display of her lack of it. There were times, it is true, that the laughter was just too loud to ignore. But even then, although she appeared upset and hurt, she dismissed the offenders as uneducated and rude, incapable of understanding her mastery. After one such humiliating situation, in a rare moment of reflection Madame Jenkins said what would become her immortal phrase: "Some people may say that I couldn't sing, but no one can say that I didn't sing."

And sing she did. Madame Jenkins was a remarkable example of a person who pursued her desire for self-expression to its ultimate consequence. The extravagance of her vision may have been a laughing matter, but it was that of someone who had refused to be inhibited by critics. She was the heroine of the untalented, those who were destined to live forever in the darkness of history because of their unremarkableness. She was a performance artist, a sum larger than its parts, a determined spirit intent on proving that the love of art could be just as powerful, if not more powerful, than the perfect execution of it. Her accompanist, McMoon, said, "When it came to singing, she forgot everything. Nothing could stop her. She thought that she was a great artist."

At her last concert, at Carnegie Hall, her artistry was not entirely lost on the critics. While reviews of the recital included the usual derisive comments, many of them had mild and polite asides. One reviewer wrote, "Everybody had a pleasant evening." Wrote another, "Her attitude was at all times that of a singer who performed her task to the best of her ability." Robert Bager of the *New York World-Telegram* observed, "She was exceedingly happy in her work. It is a pity so few artists are. And her happiness was communicated as if by magic to her listeners . . . who were stimulated to the point of audible cheering, even joyous laughter and ecstasy by the inimitable singing."

Florence died a month after that concert, on November 27, 1944. We have forgotten most of the great singers of her era, performers who were considered virtuosos in their lifetimes. But the voice and the persona of Florence Foster Jenkins has endured.

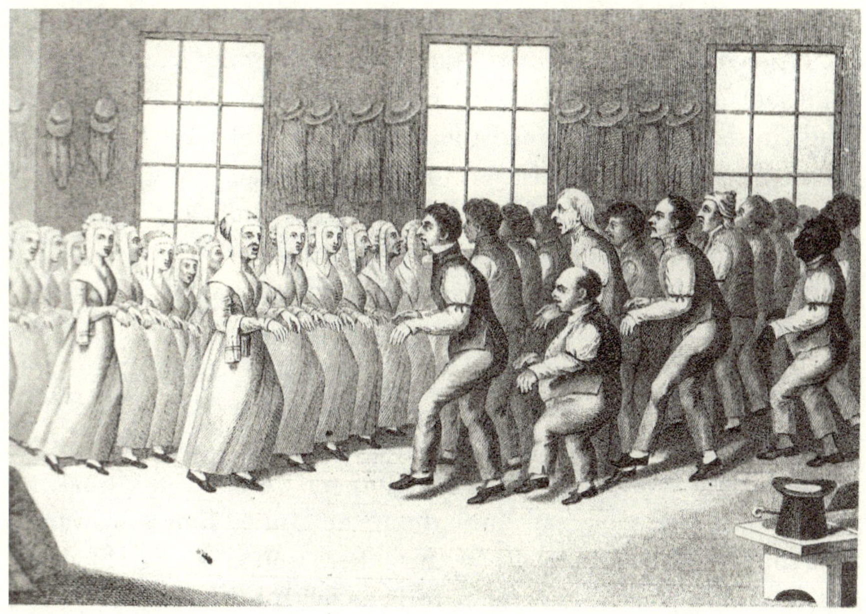

In 1774, two years before American independence, a group of people who, like Florence Jenkins, prompted mockery and ridicule fled from Manchester, England, and arrived on the shores of New York Harbor. They were a communal religious sect, known as the United Society of Believers of Christ's Second Appearing, whose religious ceremonies took the form of strenuous physical movement. Trance and vision were followed by bodily agitation, singing, dancing, and the uttering of inspired truths.

The Shakers, as they were known, described themselves as follows: "We believe we are debtors to God in relation to each other, and all men, to improve our time and talents in this life, in that manner in which we might be most useful." They also said, "Labor to make the way of God your own; let it be your inheritance, your treasure, your occupation, your daily calling."

The Shaker's movements in dance were not the only uncommon things about them. They were also led by a woman, Ann Lee. Mother Ann had had an unhappy marriage to a man her unyielding father had forced her to wed. She and her husband had four children, all of who died very young, and she found spiritual comfort in religion. When she became leader of the Shakers, Mother Ann made celibacy a requirement, and Shakers have been celibate ever since.

After two years in America, the Shakers found a piece of land in Niskayuna, now known as Watervliet, eight miles from Albany, and soon after that Mother Ann began a series of trips throughout the United States to spread the Shaker faith. Shakers benefited from the wave of revivalist sentiment that spread throughout the rural areas of the young United States, and thanks in part to the general disposition toward a new religion and to her personal determination, Mother Ann managed to convert hundreds of people to Shakerism, as far away as Kentucky.

The many-months journeys took their toll on her, and at different points in her trip she was imprisoned and accused of witchcraft. She fell ill and died at age forty-seven as a result of her hardships. But she was content, and her mission was fulfilled: the Shaker faith continued to spread throughout the United States. Toward the middle of the nineteenth century there were dozens of Shaker communities, reaching as far as Indiana, with a total of nearly six thousand members. Thanks to Mother Ann, Shakers became one of America's most successful and enduring utopian experiments.

Shakers were mocked for their anachronistic way of dressing, but it was their social and religious ideas that particularly marked them as outsiders from the traditional American society of their time. Spiritually, Shakers believe that the second coming of Christ has already taken place and is incarnated in them collectively and that they thus are already living in a new millennium. In this new coming of God all are equal, regardless of color, sex, and age, and therefore the Shakers accept converts from all ethnic groups. They are pacifists and because of that faced fierce prosecution during the War of Independence and, later on, the Civil War. Slaves who found refuge in the Shaker community gained their freedom. Thomas Jefferson once wrote of the Shakers that their socialist practices of shared property and civil disobedience would "carry us back to the times of darkest bigotry and barbarism." Abraham Lincoln had reservations about their pacifism and their request for exemption from going to war. Because Shakers are celibate, the movement grew by conversion and adoption. Shaker schools were very important in this regard, as they attracted orphans but also children "from the world" whose parents sent them there for the high quality of the education.

Traditional Shaker laws, known as the Millennial Laws, established that there should be no ornamentation in people's houses, although over the years this particular rule has relaxed somewhat. Although Shakers do not believe in the conventional notion of art, they do create artlike objects: "gift drawings," intended to be exchanged between two people. Also, Shakers document their spiritual visions. The period from 1837 to the early 1850s was very special time for them, as it saw an unusual number of visits by heavenly spirits, particularly angels, a time that became known as The Era of Manifestations. The powerful visions, known in the Shaker world as "gifts," consisted of songs, dances, images, knowledge of Heaven and of those who lived there, and instructions for the faithful about how they should act and what they should believe.

Shakers are best known for their furniture. It is not clear how such great craftsmanship started among the Shakers, but it culminated in such masterful works as the famous spiral staircase in the Shaker community in Kentucky.

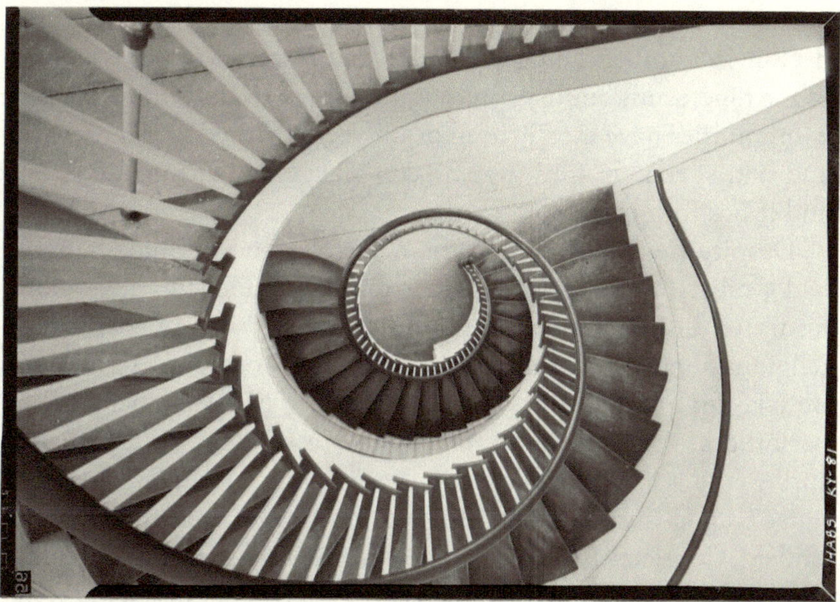

Shaker architecture is exemplary in its simplicity and practical sense. Their meeting houses are open spaces used for worship services that included singing, dancing, and praying.

The Shakers had very specific and organized choreographies for each one of their many marches, dances, and laboring songs. The singers generally remained in one area, while the other men and women moved symmetrically on either side of the meeting house. Among Shaker marches, which are no longer practiced, the earliest and most common was the Circular March: the brethren made half a circle and the sisters the other half. The vocal band stood in the middle of the circle, and the lead singer would keep the time with his foot, by stamping the floor. Shakers give particular importance to music: there are thousands of hymns, songs, and dances composed through the ages, mostly sung *a cappella.* Although Shaker songs were transmitted by oral tradition, Shakers developed nine different forms of musical notation, blending elements from traditional ballads to folk dance tunes.

With the arrival of the industrial revolution and the accompanying rapid changes in American society, the hard labor and communal life of the Shakers started to lose its appeal among potential converts. One by one, Shaker communities started to decline in numbers and grow in age, and toward the third quarter of the nineteenth century communities began to close. Now Shaker communities have mostly been destroyed or turned into museums and tourist centers. Only one Shaker village remains in operation, and it has four remaining members.

Despite their decline and their outsider status, Shakers have had a substantial impact on American life, influencing invention, furniture design, agriculture, industry, medicine, and social and religious thought. Various household and workshop items that we take for granted today were invented by Shakers, such as the flat broom, the clothespin, the circular saw blade, the automatic spring, the screw propeller, and the washing machine. The first horse wagon in the United States came from a Shaker village in Enfield, Connecticut. A Shaker in a medical shop in Mt. Lebanon, Pennsylvania, initiated the process for making condensed milk. In the waning years of World War II, when American artists were in search of a national idiom, they turned to the Shakers. Martha Graham explored the structure of their dances in *Appalachian Spring*, for which Aaron Copland composed a musical score inspired by Shaker songs like "Simple Gifts." A young Merce Cunningham performed in that legendary work.

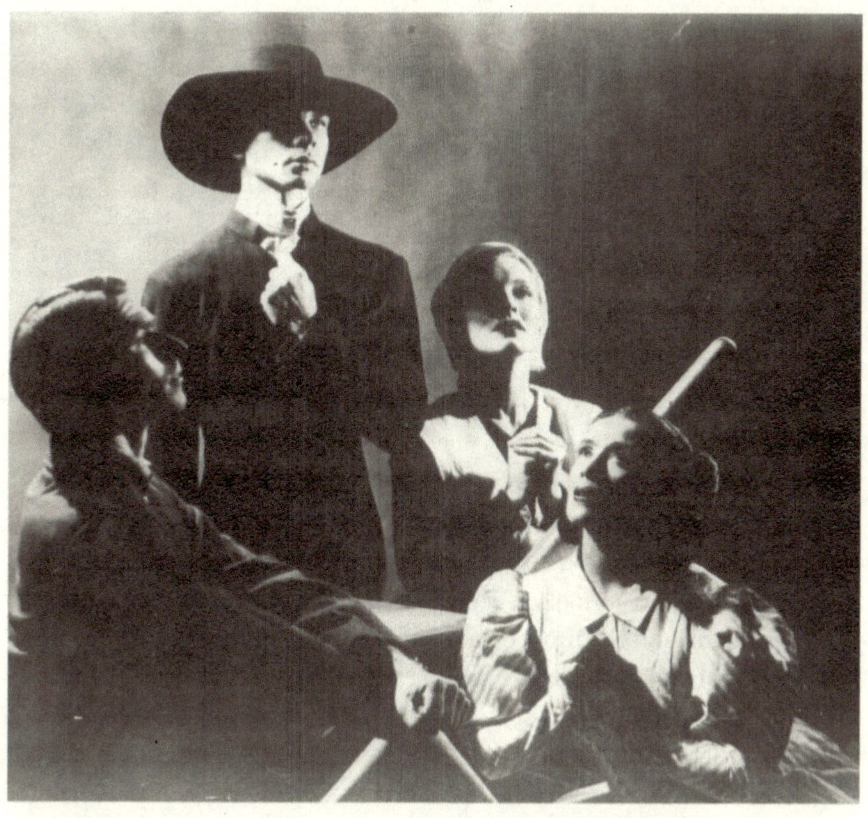

Shaker culture, which throughout the ages had been derided as eccentric, was acknowledged as a cornerstone of American identity.

I perceive unity in diversity, the correlation of forces, the interconnection of all living things, life in matter, and the principles of physics and biology.

—Friedrich Fröebel

Back in Europe, around the time the Shaker faith was first proliferating, a man started speaking about simple gifts and the importance of finding spirituality in simplicity. He, however, was interested in constructing a different kind of system for the betterment of humanity. His name was Friedrick Fröebel.

Friedrick Fröebel was born in 1782 in Oberweissbach, a small town in the principality of Schwarzburg-Rudolstaldt in central Germany, near Weimar. Born during the Enlightenment, he was a contemporary of Goethe. His mother died when he was one year old, and he was a lonely child. He had a yearning for motherly love and was sad and meditative, appropriate for the Romantic era.

Fröebel spent his adolescence with an uncle, apprenticed to a woodsman in the Turingian forest, and became versed in wood carving. He grew to be a very curious person, and quickly became interested in mathematics, crystallography, geometry, and biology. In 1811 he immersed himself in physics, mineralogy, chemistry, and natural history, and he worked at a museum of crystallography in Berlin from 1811 to 1815. Theories of biological interconnectedness fascinated Fröebel, and he soon decided that he would be an educator and devise a system for children wherein their activities would allow them to experience the unity of physical and spiritual life.

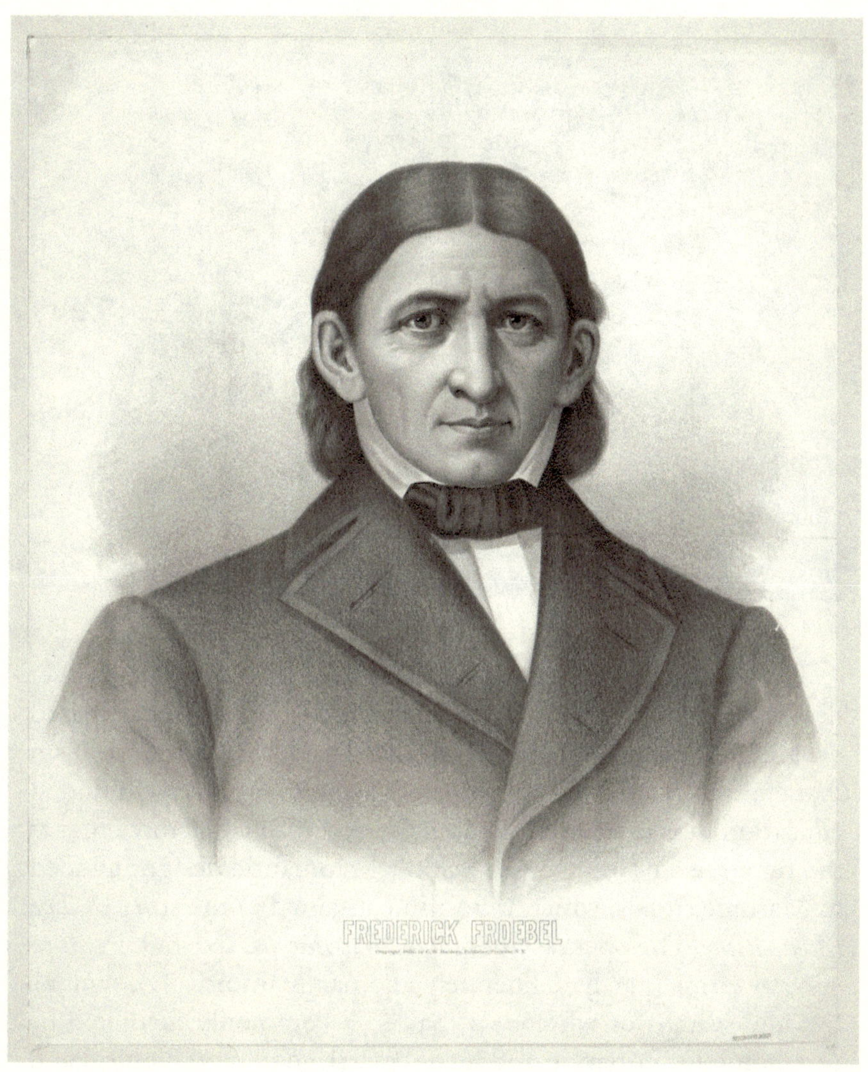
FREDERICK FROEBEL

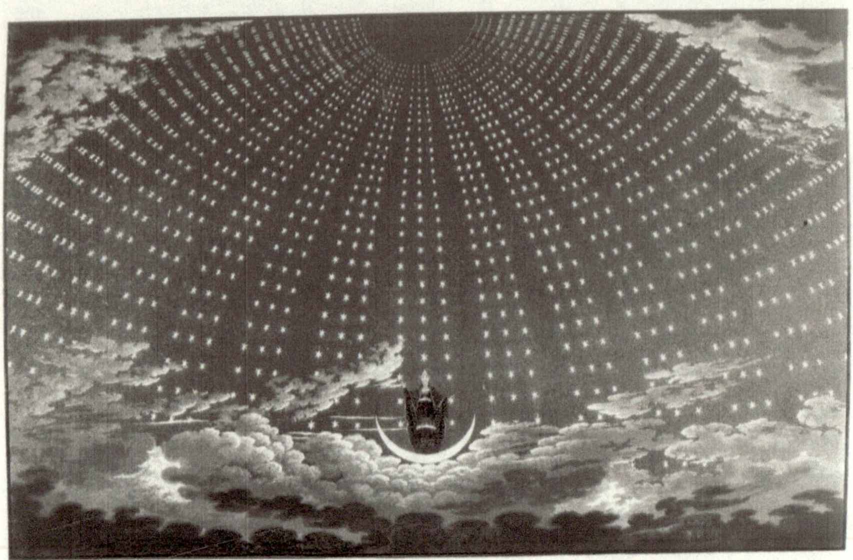

This reproduction is based on Karl Frederick Schinkel's 1819 set design for Mozart's *The Magic Flute*, the one work Mozart based on a children's tale. Schinkel's design has some of the idealism that characterizes Friedrick Fröebel's ideas about early-childhood education. It is interesting to note the occult spiritual force that at the time fueled German art. Schinkel's romantic designs alluded to Masonic rituals, which were also contained in the story of *The Magic Flute*. The opera is not only a Masonic parable but, in more general terms (partly deliberately and partly intuitively), symbolizes the search for wholeness that is so commonly furthered by ceremonies of initiation and sacred marriage in mythological and ritualistic traditions.

In Germany at that time, children did not attend school before the age of seven. Fröebel set out to devise a learning system for younger children, as he felt those to be critical years for learning. He based his theories of pedagogy on the work of Johann Heinrich Pestalozzi, who supported a more creative approach than recitation by memory. He called his system *Kindergarten*, or "garden for children," a play on words that referred to the idea of free recreation in a nourishing and a welcoming environment.

The first kindergarten opened in 1837. According to Fröebel, the kindergarten method satisfied

> *1. The need for physical movement through playing; 2. A child's need to occupy oneself in a plastic fashion, through projects that help develop dexterity of the senses; 3. A child's need to develop artistic faculties; 4. A child's need to know; 5. A child's need to cultivate and take care for something; 6. A child's need to sing, to produce aesthetic taste; 7. The need to live in society; and 8. The greatest need of all: to find God.*

How did he accomplish this? Fröebel spent his life devising activities he described as "gifts," objects for children to play with in various activities. This eventually led to what is probably Fröebel's most famous invention: building blocks used to create various architectural forms.

In his work *The Education of Man*, published in 1826, Fröebel expressed the importance of building blocks as simple playthings that allow children to

> *feel and experience, to act and represent, to think and recognize. Building, aggregation, is instinctive in the child; it is essential in the development of mankind. The importance of the vertical, the horizontal, and the rectangular is the first experience the child gathers from building; then follow equilibrium and symmetry. Thus the child ascends from the construction of the simplest wall to the more complex and even to the invention of every architectural structure.*

Other gifts are based on colored parquetry paper and paper sticks, folding projects, and combinations of drawing and building geometric forms. For Fröebel, the purpose of drawing was to help children visualize how forms are constructed—for example, that a star is the combination of various triangles. Fröebel's system usually consisted in drawing from nature followed by a step-by-step progression to the least representational forms.

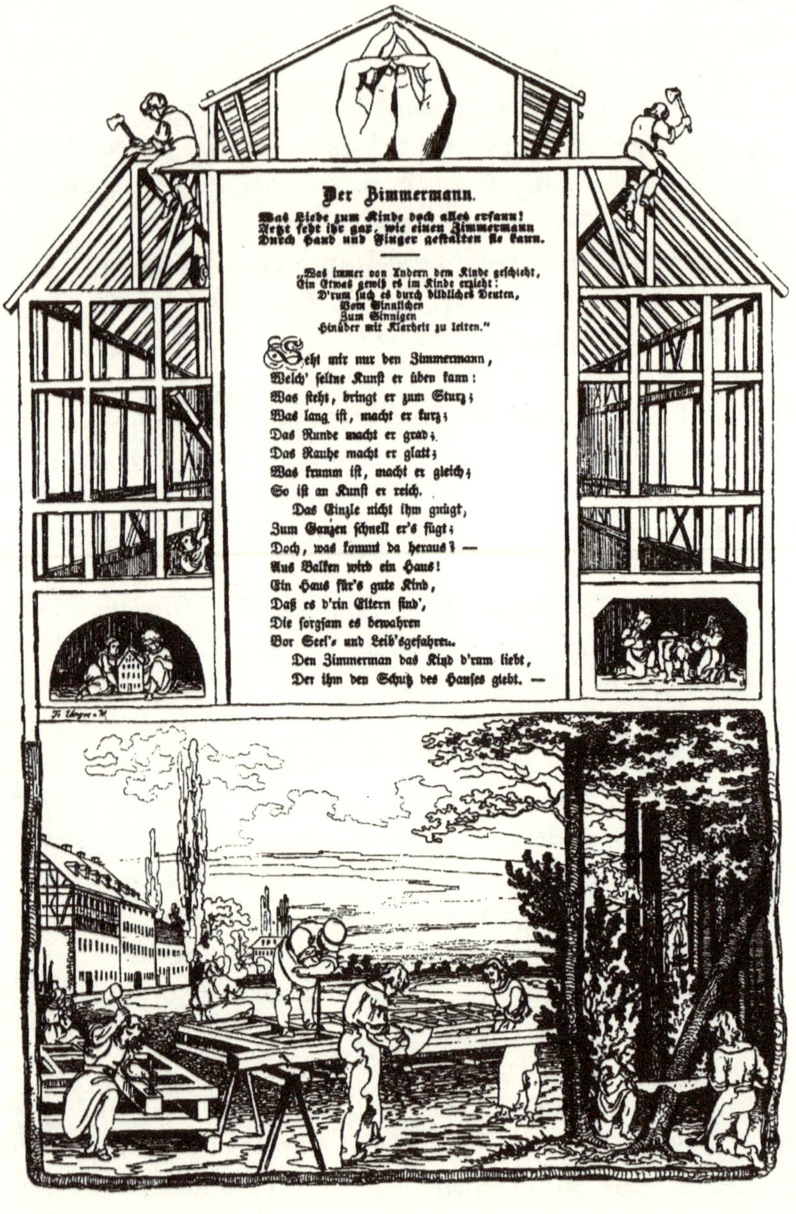
Der Zimmermann.
Was Liebe zum Kinde doch alles ersann!
Jetzt seht ihr gar, wie einen Zimmermann
Durch Hand und Finger gestalten sie kann.
„Was immer von Andern dem Kinde geschieht,
Ein Etwas gewiß es im Kinde erzieht:
D'rum such es durch bildliches Deuten,
Vom Sinnlichen
Zum Sinnigen
Hinüber mit Klarheit zu leiten."
Seht mir nur den Zimmermann,
Welch' seltne Kunst er üben kann:
Was steht, bringt er zum Sturz;
Was lang ist, macht er kurz;
Das Runde macht er grad;
Das Rauhe macht er glatt;
Was krumm ist, macht er gleich;
So ist an Kunst er reich.
Das Einzle nicht ihm genügt,
Zum Ganzen schnell er's fügt;
Doch, was kommt da heraus? —
Aus Balken wird ein Haus!
Ein Haus für's gute Kind,
Daß es d'rin Eltern find',
Die sorgsam es bewahren
Vor Seel'- und Leib'sgefahren.
Den Zimmerman das Kind d'rum liebt,
Der ihm den Schutz des Hauses giebt. —

Friedrich Fröebel's *Mutter und Kofe-lieder* (*Mother-Play and Nursery Songs*), first published in 1844, is the most popular and influential book he wrote. It includes more than fifty simple songs and games for mothers to play with their children. Each song in *Mother-Play* comes with music (lyrics with traditional folk tunes), a picture illustrating a simple concept or lesson, and a motto or short commentary for the mother. They were later adopted in other countries, such as in American kindergartens.

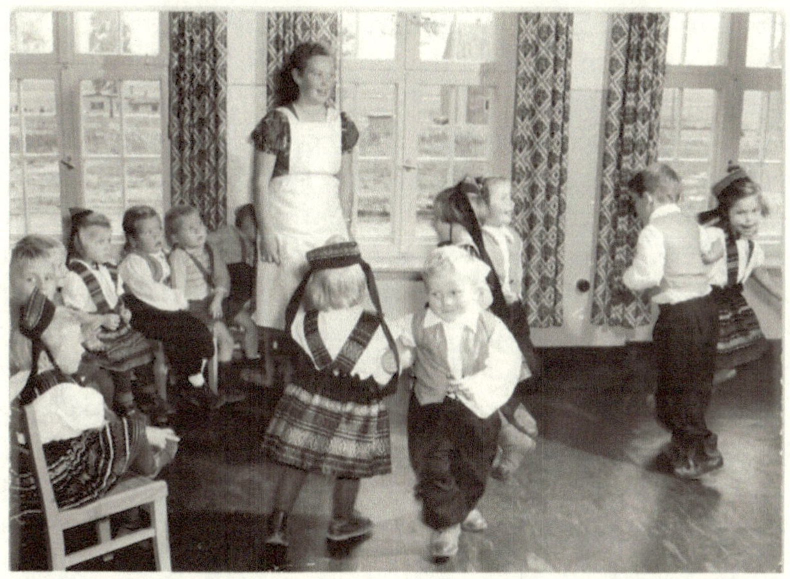

Music and group singing are essential to Fröebel's kindergarten: classes start and end with a song or dance. Fröebel valued songs with simple, even nonsensical lyrics as potent means for nontraditional communication.

Despite the early popularity of kindergarten, Fröebel did not live to see the real proliferation of his school. Due to a combination of unfortunate circumstances and politics, the Prussian government prohibited kindergarten teaching. This was a fatal blow to Fröebel, who died one year later, in 1852, thinking that his system had failed.

Yet nothing could be further from the truth. A group of German educators who strongly believed in Fröebel's system went all around Europe, Russia, and the United States spreading his method. Within thirty years, the kindergarten methodology was strongly established in modern education. The first kindergarten in the United States was founded in Watertown, Wisconsin, by Margaret Schurz, a German immigrant, in 1856. In 1873 the first public-school kindergarten opened in Manitowoc, Wisconsin. There teacher Ruth Burrit's experimental class attracted the attention of Anna Lloyd Wright. Mrs. Wright wanted her son to be an architect and studied the kindergarten technique to teach her children at home.

Many years later, the greatest architect of the twentieth century would refer to this as a critical aspect of his creative development and would credit Fröebel's system as the foundation of his architecture. In his various Taliesin lectures, Frank Lloyd Wright said, "Mother learned that Friedrick Fröebel taught that children should not be allowed to draw from casual appearances of nature until they had mastered the basic forms lying behind appearances. Cosmic, geometric elements were what should first be made visible to the child-mind."

Thus was born a sensibility toward the union of geometry and nature that would be widely shared by the generation of artists who led the avant-garde movements of the twentieth century. "Form, and whatever may depend on form, reveals in various ways inner spiritual energy." Frederick Fröebel said these words, so similar to Piet Mondrian's manifesto of Neo-Plasticism, in 1826, nearly one hundred years before Mondrian, as historian and writer Norman Brosterman has pointed out.

What is the relationship between art, education, spirituality, and personal experience?

What is the connection between art and experience?

Art history became living history for me when I met Ward Jackson.

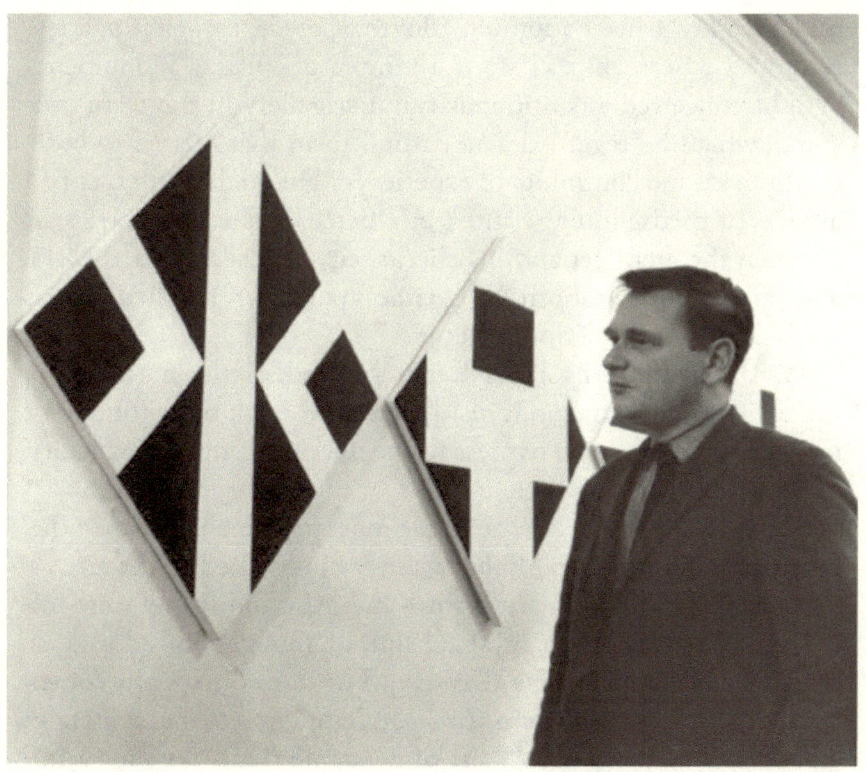

My name is Pablo Helguera. I moved to New York in 1998 and got a job in the education department of the Guggenheim museum. My office was located in an annex to the museum, known as the Liederkrantz, which houses a German lieder society founded in 1847. It also contains the entire archives of the Guggenheim. My office was adjacent to that of a quiet man, someone, I was told, named Ward Jackson, the archivist of the museum and the longest-working staff person in the history of the institution.

Ward Jackson was a teenager in Petersburg, Virginia, when he first learned about Solomon R. Guggenheim's Museum of Non-objective Painting. In the 1940s he wrote a letter to Guggenheim's art advisor, Hilla von Rebay, who invited him to visit her while he was in New York. Around that time Rebay commissioned Frank Lloyd Wright to design a new building for what would become the Solomon R. Guggenheim Museum. In a famous letter, Rebay told Wright, "I need a fighter, a lover of space, an agitator, a tester and a wise man . . . I want a temple of spirit, a monument." Wright conceived a continuous running gallery in the form of a spiral, which he regarded as a natural form that related to both multiplicity and continuity of experience. This and other eccentric aspects of the building resulted in a fierce debate and a struggle between the architect and his clients, city officials, the art world, and public opinion. Both Guggenheim and Wright died before the building's completion in 1959.

Ward was hired by Hilla Rebay to work at the museum, in the registrar department, in 1955. He would work there for nearly forty years, becoming a witness to the development of the history of American art.

Vassily Kandinsky was one of the most prominent artists in the museum's collection, and Rebay was very influenced by the artist's ideas of the spiritual in art. Both Kandinsky and Rebay were followers of Theosophy, a mystical line of thought introduced in Russia by Madame Helena Blavatsky. The term Theosophy comes from the Neo-Platonic term *theosophia*, employed to mean, literally, "knowledge of the divine." One of Madame Blavatsky's most important maxims was "Compassion is the law of laws." She explained that brotherhood is not a mere ideal—it is a fact in nature and it exists on the spiritual plane. From that she derived a logical basis and a binding source for a guiding morality. Theosophy, according to Blavatsky, is a synonym of *eternal truth.* The new torchbearer of truth, according to her, will find the minds of men prepared for his message: "Earth will be Heaven in the twenty-first century, compared to what it is now."

When Ward Jackson moved to New York, a generation of American artists were questioning the nature of what modern American art should express. They had lived through World War II and afterward experienced a profound period of self-examination that perhaps has not yet been repeated.

This was when Aaron Copland and Martha Graham collaborated on *Appalachian Spring*, based on Shaker tunes and dances. In the visual arts, Abstract Expressionism was an emphatic expression of an American idiom. Agnes Martin, Ad Reinhardt, and other abstract artists pursued a sort of spirituality in their work. These pure forms were deeply influential in the development of Ward Jackson's artwork, which is in the collection of the Guggenheim Museum. A shy person, Ward would not talk to me at first. He finally opened up one day after I found him having trouble with the office copier and helped him make some photocopies. We started a series of elevator conversations, usually when we coincided in exiting the building. Gradually he told me about Jackson Pollock and his times working at the Guggenheim, the time de Kooning took him out for a spaghetti dinner, the character of Hilla Rebay, his feeling that no one cared anymore about real abstraction, and taking care of the archives of an institution.

Jackson is a member of the American Association of Abstract Artists, a group that promotes and discusses the value of American abstract art. In addition to de Kooning, he was friends with many important American artists, including Dan Flavin. Flavin had a practice of dedicating individual works to family, friends, or historical figures of significance to him, and Ward was especially significant. His 1971 installation for the Guggenheim is called *untitled* (*to Ward Jackson, an old friend and colleague who, during the Fall of 1957 when I finally returned to New York from Washington and joined him to work together in this museum, kindly communicated*).

The last time I saw Ward, he had retired but continued to walk around the offices of the museum like a ghost from an earlier era. He still refers to the museum as a "temple of spirit," the words of Hilla Rebay to Wright.

I ask myself how much of the initial idealist spirit of modern art still remains in us, after all. But most significantly, Ward regarded that museum as a transformative environment grounded on powerful, spiritual forces. Was it a deluded view, or is there truly a relationship between physical spaces and the ability to create transcendental experiences?

Perhaps the answer to that can be found in the story of a man who lived five hundred years ago.

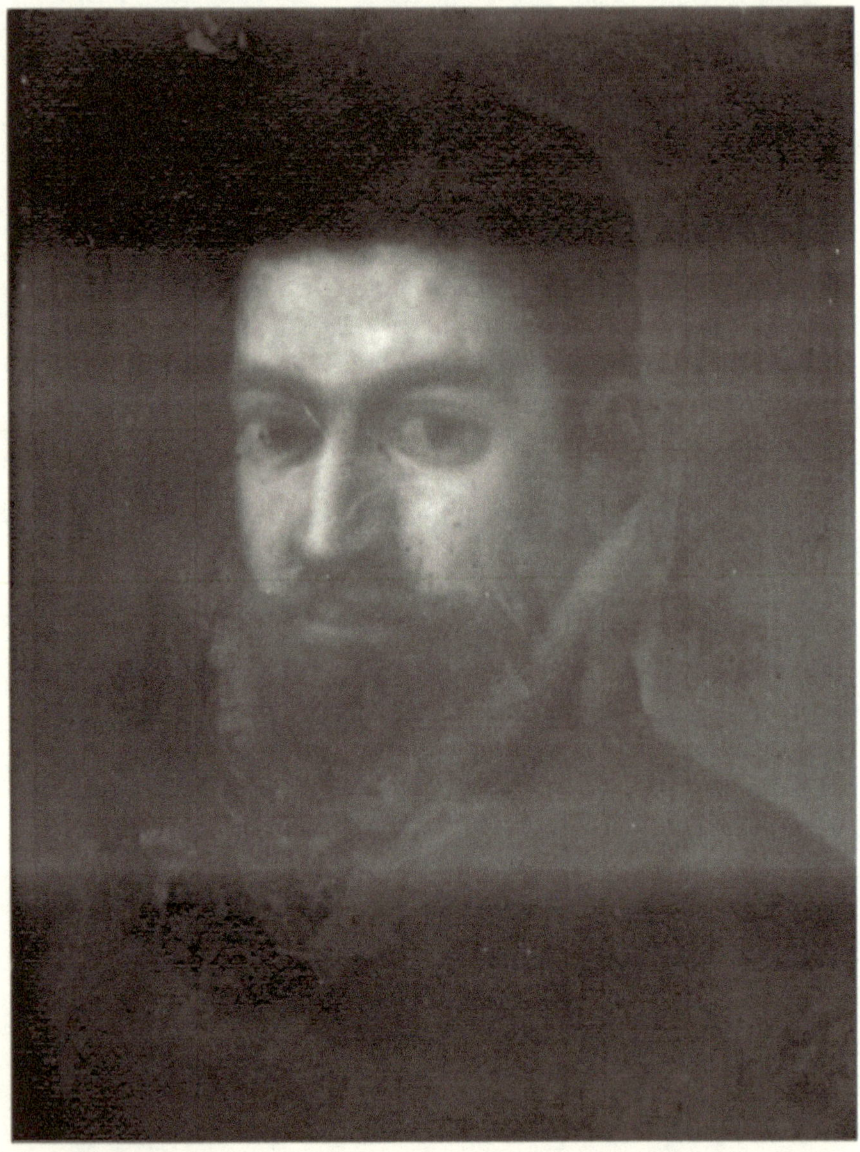

Giulio Camillo Delminio gained widespread renown in Europe in the beginning of the sixteenth century, yet much about him was shrouded in secrecy. It was rumored that he had built a theater with magical qualities, a place of transformative powers. The secret of how it really worked was revealed only to the king of France. What was it exactly?

In 1532 in Padua, Viglius Zuichemus told his friend Erasmus of Rotterdam in a letter describing the enthusiastic talk around this man named Giulio Camillo: "They say that this man has constructed a sort of Amphitheater, a work of wonderful skill; whoever enters as spectator will be able to discourse on any subject no less fluently than Cicero. . . . Figures are set in certain orders or grades . . . with stupendous labor and divine skill."

Erasmus, the leading intellectual of the time, asked Viglius to find out more. Viglius eventually met Camillo and saw his theater in Italy. On their first encounter Viglius was underwhelmed: the man was not quite the all-knowing figure he claimed his theater would produce. A short, nervous, and shy person, he stuttered and spoke broken Latin, which he attributed to a speech impediment.

Camillo was a practitioner of the ancient art of memory, which had its roots in Greece around 500 BC, the time of the poet Simonides of Ceos. Simonides had developed a visual formula for remembering long texts, in which the speaker imagines an architectural space with several rooms in which he "places" different images associated with the different parts of the text. By visualizing the various rooms, he could easily retrieve the "stored" information.

This practice continued to be developed into the Middle Ages, as summarized by the Latin phrase *constat igitur artificiosa memoria ex locis et imaginibus*—"artificial memory is established from the conjunction of places and images." The practice was mostly useful for students of oratory and rhetoric, but somewhere around the time of the medieval Catalan philosopher Ramon Lull the practice of the art of memory started acquiring esoteric dimensions. The way it was perceived by certain occultist and Neo-Platonist philosophers, this practice would allow one not just to *remember* but to *attain* divine knowledge. This was the art of memory Camillo pursued. He thought he could build a place where all the things of the world could be known, both human and divine. He called it Memory Theater.

Every structural element had a symbolic role in Camillo's system.

According to him, by using an associative combination of the emblematically coded division of knowledge, it would be possible to reproduce every imaginable universal relationship in one's own memory. Exactly how this would work remained a mystery, with the key to it hidden somewhere in the many symbols of hermetic occult sciences and Jewish mysticism on which Camillo based his notions.

Geometric relationships were an important element of memory systems and hermetic thought. Mystics like Camillo continuously established relationships between one idea and another, based on the general notion that divine unity comprises all things. Such systems were known as *ars combinatoria*, or combinatory art. The wheel of the Seven Source Spirits, for example, shows the basic structure of the process of nature, the eternal in-and-out folding of the divine underground, and the miraculous eye of eternity. Camillo, like the Theosophists later, described God as a wheel with seven inner wheels, constituting the Seven Spirits of God, forever giving birth to one another.

Whoever entered the theater would symbolically operate the machinery of the cosmos, which was theoretically controlled by legions of angels, and so, metaphorically, turn into an angel himself. The theater depicted the various stages of Creation, from the "first cause" (that is, the primal force of the universe), through the angels, the planetary spheres, and down to Man. The dark background of the skies represented the hidden aspect of God. Once Man sees himself reflected in the mirror of Heaven, according to Camillo, he "will impregnate itself with imagination from wisdom." In a way, Camillo's theater was a means for having a spiritual vision of the universe.

Despite his explanations, neither Viglius nor Erasmus were convinced of the viability of Camillo's project. New European intellectuals like them were more inclined to scientific rigor and distrusted the use of the art of memory as some sort of suspicious magic, and Hermetism was seen as an old-fashioned and useless practice. In the end, Camillo did not get the intellectual support he needed, the king of France did not give him much-needed funding, and the theater was never finished.

Before Camillo died, he wrote a text known as *L'Idea del teatro*, describing his project for posterity. But as it turned out, ironically, the man who wanted to create a universal memory system eventually became virtually forgotten. It wasn't until the 1960s that British historian Frances Yates rescued Camillo's writings from obscurity and tried to reconstruct his memory theater. For all the eccentricity that Camillo's ideas appeared to have among his intellectual contemporaries, and although his ideas were rooted in obscure practices even in his time, he may have been onto something that is now very familiar to us. In his monumental attempt to create a system of visual representation of the impossible complexity of the world, he was, perhaps, the very first person in history to try to construct a virtual interface. Camillo's description of a place where all thoughts can be seen and known resembles very closely our digital utopias of knowledge, particularly the concept of the search engine. Camillo was, in a way, the first person to conceive of Google.

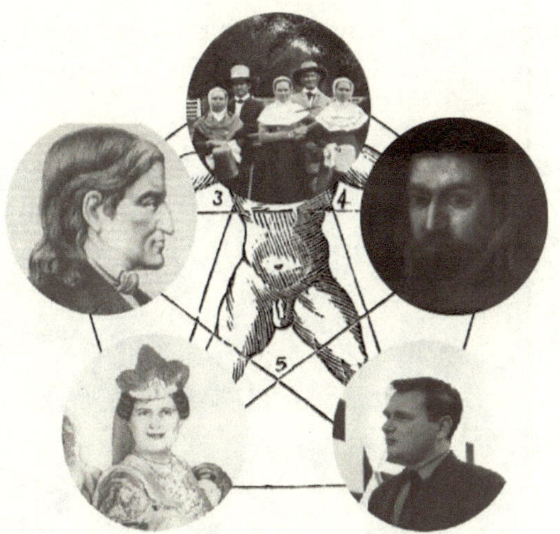

So, you may ask what all of this means.

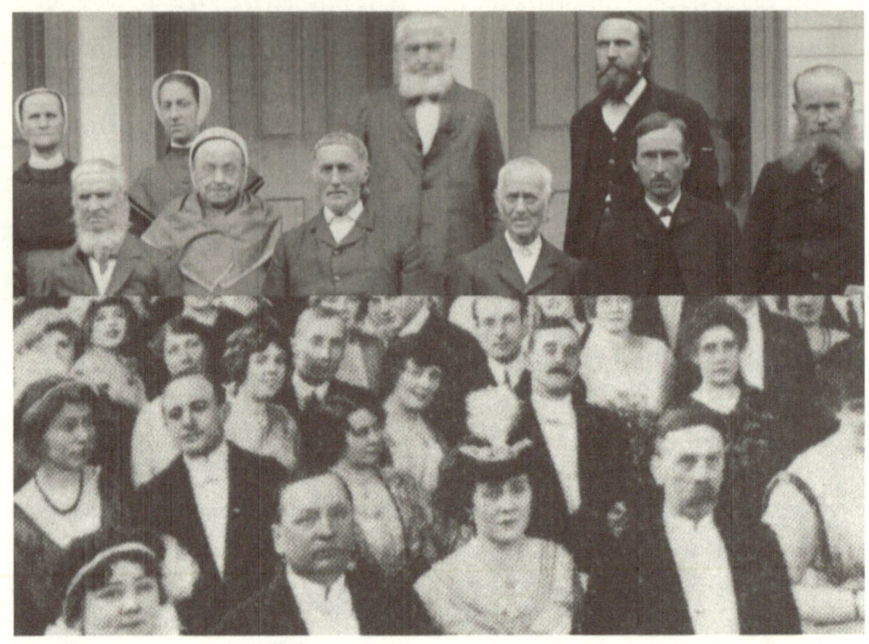

Perhaps it means that although certain lives appear to be failures, they are always redeemed by the nobility of their efforts.

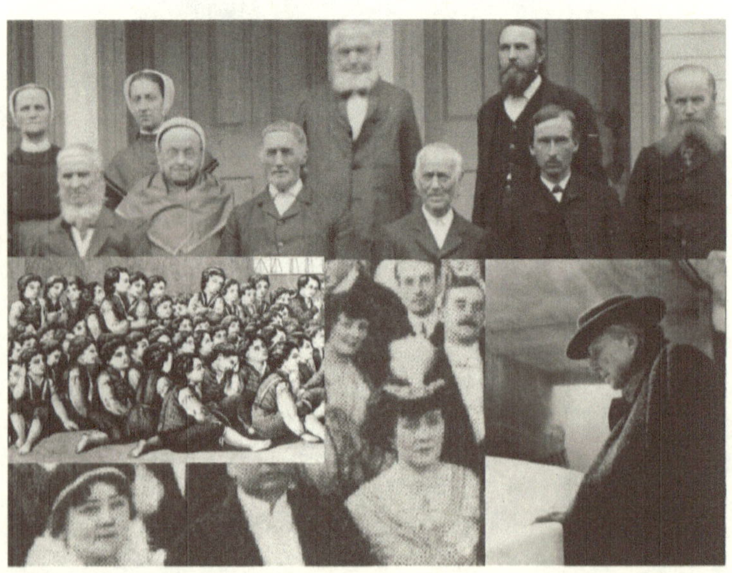

Perhaps it means that imprinting an indelible message in the minds of others is a high task and may be the product of a very strong belief, but it is always an endeavor of love.

Perhaps it means that we can only be measured in what we have done for others, or perhaps that there is greatness in pursuing things that appear unnecessary to others,

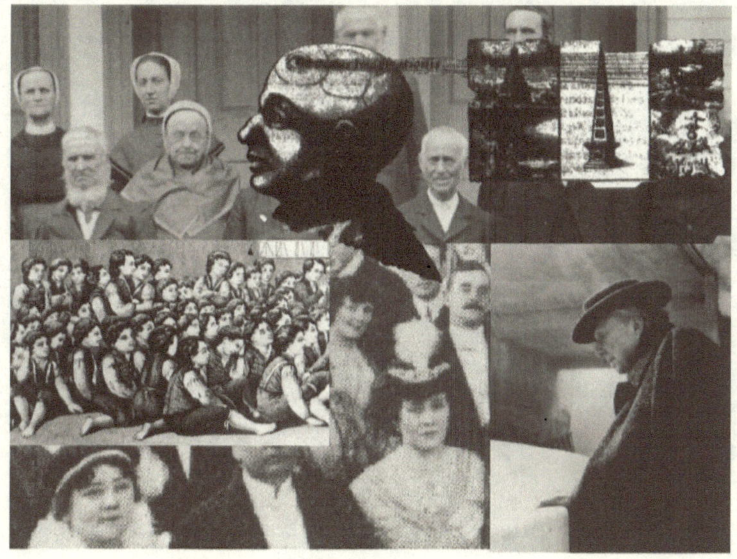

and perhaps that those who live anachronistic lives may sometimes appear profoundly stupid, yet what they understand may go beyond patterns of clarity,

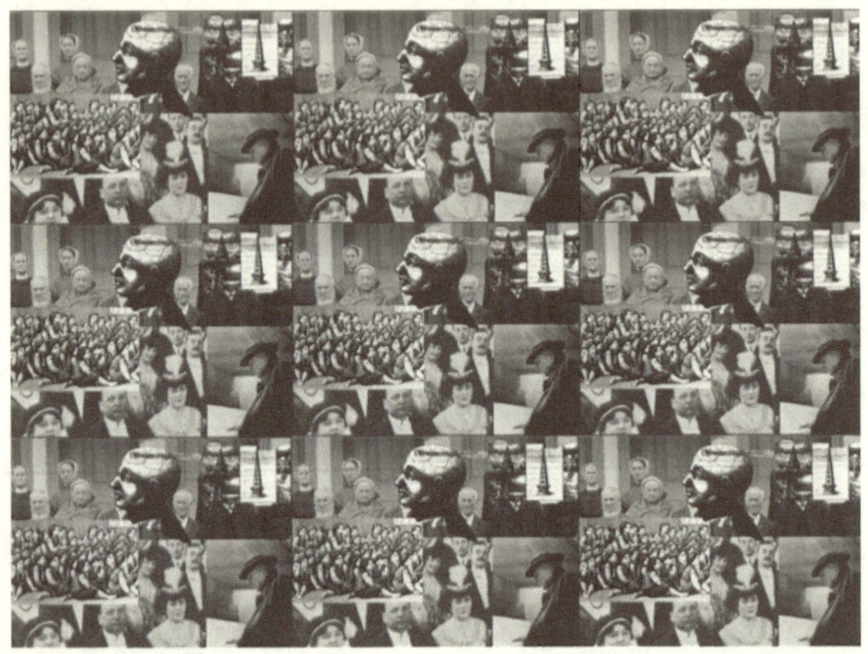

and that perhaps, indeed, we all are others, as much as we all are ourselves.

The First Imaginary Forum of Mental Sculpture (2004)

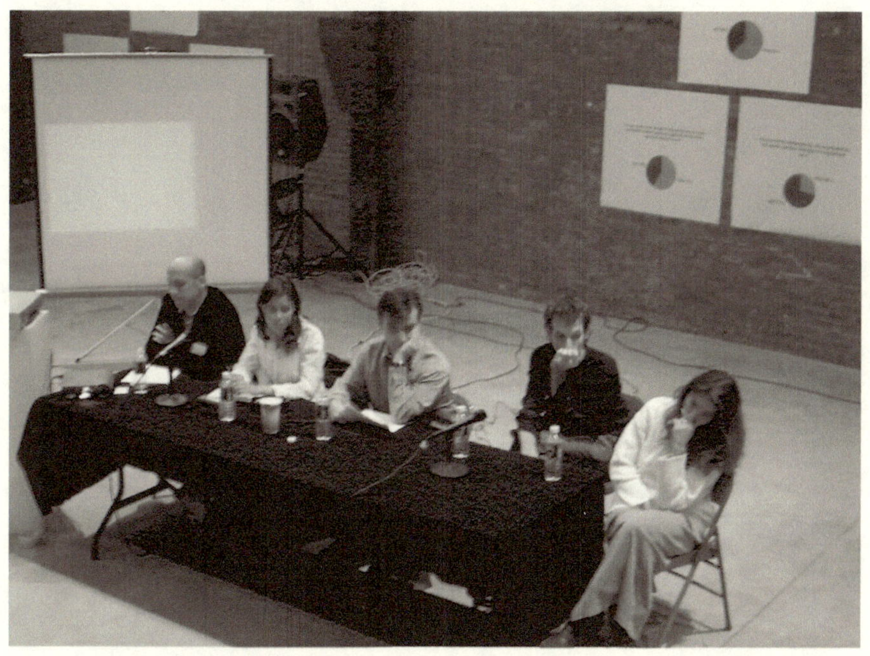

On October 2, 2004, the Sculpture Center, El Museo del Barrio, and the Hermetic Lounge in New York presented The First Imaginary Forum of Mental Sculpture, organized by Pablo Helguera. The Imaginary Forum's publicity and program notes claimed that it sought to improve the quality of academic and theoretical debate and went on to say that the Forum reserved the right to use "undisclosed theatrical devices" to accomplish its goals. Despite this phrase in the publicity and program notes, the fact that this could have been a scripted event escaped most of the audience, and at the end there were a wide variety of perceptions among the audience about the nature of the event, including whether it had been a real panel discussion or a performance. At any rate, most agreed that the debate between audience and actors had been surprisingly lively, and their engagement in the discussion was singularly intense. Audience member Patrick Killoran wrote: "[the event] rode the edge of reality just enough to keep me in a daze all night. I am not sure I like the idea of being clueless for more than a day or two, but in a way it does not matter."

The script was written based on the results of a poll about art-world issues conducted a few weeks before the event.

APPEARING

Josko Andric, based in New York. Very young and successful artist originally from Bosnia. Sort of an Anri Sala type. Scrubby, the image of introverted genius. Looks like a model, dressed in black. Mid-to-late twenties

Pablo Helguera, moderator

Holly McKenley, art critic. She is in her late forties/early fifties. Marxist. Unkempt, no makeup

Brian T. Morgan, writer. Mid-forties

Patricia Ortiz de Montellano, curator/gallerist. Curator of a prominent Latin-American collection in Buenos Aires, originally from Barcelona. Extremely attractive, early thirties, Armani suit, impeccable, and fashionable

Two audience members

The panel takes place at the Sculpture Center in New York on October 2, 2004, nearly a month after the anniversary of 9/11 and a few weeks before the presidential election.

Pablo Helguera

Ladies and gentlemen, thank you for coming tonight to the Sculpture Center. This event, the First Imaginary Forum of Mental Sculpture, has been organized by the Hermetic Lounge, an artist organization that seeks to promote public debate and compile opinion about the contemporary art world.

This panel focuses on the role of art in contemporary society and politics, a topical subject these days given the electoral climate in the United States and the current international situation.

We are gathered here to discuss how academia and the art market could turn art into a dynamic agent of change in our society instead of merely a commodity. This project originated from the collective feeling that contemporary art has become quite a marginal voice in the larger public dialogue on politics. So, taking as an inspiration the work of Joseph Beuys, who promoted an idea of collective discussion once described as "mental sculpture," we are here to discuss how we can make art relevant again.

In the interest of saving time, and per request of the participants, I will forego long introductions of the panelists. But very briefly I will present them to you: Josko Andric is a prominent artist, originally from Bosnia, who has been featured at the Venice Biennale and many other prominent international exhibitions. Patricia Ortiz de Montellano is a curator and the director of the Garza collection in Buenos Aires, which is one of the most important collections of contemporary art in Latin America. She is on the board of various contemporary art institutions. Brian T. Morgan has written eight books on contemporary art theory and is a regular contributor to *Art in America*, *Frieze*, and *Artforum*. Holly McKenley is a critic and self-described art activist, founder of the group Art for Action in the late 1970s, and currently a professor of feminism and art history at the University of Georgia. She has published widely on contemporary art and politics since 1977.

We are living in a time of anxiety and frustration in the art world. There is a recurrent debate amongst art publications and scholarly circles around the topic that contemporary art does not communicate effectively with the public about significant political issues and that contemporary art practice is unable to instigate substantial social change. Tonight we will discuss such issues and we will hear from our panelists about ways to address them.

In order to initiate a discussion, the Hermetic Lounge conducted an opinion poll about a number of issues that will occupy us tonight. The pollsters questioned a cross-section of the international art world, including curators, artists, collectors, critics, and audience members from Slovakia to New York. The first two polls show that 79 percent of the art world feels that most contemporary art does not contribute to political dialogue in a significant way. The second, perhaps more interesting finding is that the art world is basically divided on whether people are more motivated by personal agendas or genuine interest in art.

I would like to start this discussion by asking the group: What do you think about the statement that the art world is out of touch with international and local politics? And, second, if people did put their personal agendas ahead of a genuine interest in art, would social and political issues become secondary concerns in the art world?

Brian T. Morgan

This is a subject that I addressed in 1996 in my book *The End of Political Art*, which some in the audience may be familiar with. In the book I analyze how we are part of a long philosophical crisis in art. Part of this crisis, as I tried to prove, is our inability to find a model of art making that would be both visually significant and accessible, enter into an intelligent dialogue with modernism and politics, and, most importantly, have a physical presence in museums and galleries. This is not to say that there weren't groups of artists that tried to instigate social change, but their effectiveness was limited at best. They just have not been able to overcome the market model of art, which supports but at the same time stifles creativity.

Holly McKenley

First, I want to thank Pablo for bringing us together to discuss this issue, which I do consider a very important one to address. I personally do not agree that we have been unable to produce significant art that has influenced politics, but I do believe that the economic structure of the art world has made it very difficult to make a kind of art that is independent and does not submit to the necessity of being bought. Museums are indeed a problem because they are collections of objects—and for a regular museum visitor, the physicality of the object is unconsciously important. We see a lot of very large paintings, but we don't see the actions and performances that took place in the same period; thus the unconscious sense is that any given period of art making was dominated by object-oriented art.

Patricia Ortiz de Montellano

Well, I think it's just a matter of education. I think the more you know about contemporary art, the more art fairs you have been to, the more biennials, you would be able to identify the issues raised by artists.

McKenley

But isn't that an elitist position?

Ortiz de Montellano

I don't think so. If you think of art as science, for instance—scientists are supposed to know a lot, and scientific texts are not intended to be understood by everyone. There are things that you just cannot simplify. I think one just has to get involved in the art world.

Plus, I want to say that I do think there are a lot of interesting artists, such as Josko Andric, who is here with us today, whose work does deal with social issues and has been included in a lot of significant exhibitions, such as the last Venice Biennale.

Helguera
Perhaps Josko, you would like to show some of your work and discuss it in terms of the issues raised here? I know you've brought a video . . .

Josko Andric
Yes, thanks a lot. I guess I will start with some background information about me and my work. I was born and raised in Bosnia-Herzegovina, which I left during the beginning of the Balkan war. I was always interested in being an artist and felt it was necessary to express through my work the traumatic feelings that result from human conflict.

(*The video starts playing. It shows someone's foot leaning against a windowsill, and someone putting on and taking off a number of socks*).

This video that I am showing right now was made for the Venice Biennale, and it illustrates conflict between religious communities. You see, there is a character trying on a number of socks. All these socks belong to dead soldiers in the Balkan war, I mean, they were taken from the feet of dead soldiers and put in a place where they would be reused by others, as there was a shortage of clothing. This is a person trying a variety of these socks.

Ortiz de Montellano
I just want to say that this work of Josko is a really eloquent reflection on human conflict, and it's a good example of what I mean when I say that there is a lot of interesting political art out there with a strong and powerful message.

McKenley
Well, actually, I am not sure how political the piece is. Not to sound offensive, but I think we have a different idea of what "political art" means. This work just illustrates a situation of some sort, but it doesn't say anything about it, nor does the situation refer by itself to what you say it does. And, to be honest, that's a large part of the

problem I have with contemporary art today: the press release says that it "explores" this or "investigates" this or that subject, but at the end of the day you don't know what it's actually saying about it. I mean, when you say someone "explores" a subject, what does that actually mean? What is the work actually saying about it?

I say this because this work is to me just illustrating some random action. To claim that it is some sort of political statement is a stretch at best.

Andric
Like I said, it's depicting the tensions, the social tensions . . . the sense of absence . . . there is a sense of existential emptiness that interests me . . . and I really don't expect everyone to see what I see in the piece.

Ortiz de Montellano
I think it is really clear, what Josko is doing—his video brings attention to an issue that many of us are not aware of. Again, it is about educating the public.

Morgan
It is true that some background is required in order to understand the message of political art, but it is also true that politics is something that we are all familiar with to some extent. You may not know where those socks came from, but if you are intrigued enough and you learn what they are, the piece changes for you. Hegel said—

McKenley
(*Interrupting*) Excuse me, but frankly I think that we too often get trapped in definitions and interpretations while, ironically, actually looking at the substance of the work falls by the wayside. I am amazed that more people don't see this, but I think that a lot of political art, or art that is self-proclaimed as political, is just a formula for elegant videos about issues that are certain to have a wide appeal—but that is very different from making a work that really impacts and changes society.

Andric
Well, in all honesty, as an artist, I really am not concerned about what the public will say. I mean, it would constrain my creativity. I think that as artists we should just create, and if there is interest in it, great; and if not, so be it. An artist makes a heartfelt statement, and I think that is enough.

Ortiz de Montellano
I think that works like these do definitely have an impact—they have been seen by thousands of people.

Helguera
Do you think it's possible to verify the kind of social impact the work has had toward that specific cause?

Ortiz de Montellano
I am sorry, and I am perhaps on the wrong panel here, but I just don't see why we place so much importance on the political message in art. I mean, art is not just about politics; it is art, not politics.

Andric
In answer to your question, I think all art always has some sort of impact, and that always benefits the public no matter how. And I think it's always good to make art, regardless of what it is about.

Helguera
I would like to bring up another poll: eighty-three percent of the art world seems to think that profiting financially from denouncing a political or social injustice is ethical. Any thoughts about that?

McKenley
You can certainly verify the economic impact, which is another subject that I find problematic about this kind of work. You make a documentary piece about suffering people in, say, the Iraq war, or 9/11, showing dead bodies or people whose family members were killed. Then the work is admired and bought by an important collector. What kind of good does it do to the people the piece is

documenting, and what happens when a supposedly "critical" social piece is bought, enhancing the reputation of the artist, making him rich? Who is really benefiting from that?

Morgan
OK, but can you give some examples of works that do not exploit causes? Should artists do work about nothing, for that reason?

McKenley
Of course I can: a lot of artwork from the sixties and seventies, activist art that raised important awareness of feminist and racial issues.

Ortiz de Montellano
Well, I think that now we live in the twenty-first century, and we really have changed a lot in our way of understanding human conflict, we have become a bit more sophisticated in the art world in how we debate certain kinds of issues . . . In the seventies we were more idealistic, and that really didn't get us anywhere.

McKenley
We have become more cynical. We pat ourselves on the back when we are admiring works that supposedly are about suffering and human injustice, and yet we use the money that could aid those causes to throw parties that cost millions of dollars. It suffices to share a few figures I read just yesterday, which also have been made public by the Hermetic Lounge. (*She looks at her papers.*) For instance, the opening party for the American Pavilion at the Venice Biennale cost a quarter of a million dollars. I don't think I have to go into how this money could be used to benefit social and political causes instead of providing entertainment to the artistic elite.

Morgan
There is a lot written about "white guilt" in the art world. We tell each other that we support causes so that we feel better about them. But there are two critical points here: the activity of making art

can never replace the activity of being a social worker or a political agent; those who want to really influence politics directly should perhaps just become politicians and not artists.

(*Josko and Patricia nod in approval.*)

On the other hand, as artists we can't help but talk about the social and political issues that happen around us. To pretend they don't exist would throw us back to a Kantian understanding of the art object as simply a beautiful piece, as some universe of its own. So it seems to me that we have a divide here in the art world, two positions that I find a bit dogmatic in their own way: one that thinks of the art world as something separate from the rest of the world; and the other that seems to believe it can really change the world.

Ortiz de Montellano
I think there is a third way, which is to construct pretentious theoretical notions about art without really experiencing the art world in real life and get credit for presenting contemporary art as a world in crisis. Why can't people just accept that there is great art out there that can just be enjoyed?

McKenley
I have a few questions for Josko, which perhaps can aid this discussion. Josko, when did you start making art?

Andric
What do you mean, when I started? I was producing my own videos in Bosnia . . . I was trying to make musical videos . . .

McKenley
And then what happened?

Andric
Well, the war started, and I moved to Paris . . . I showed one of my videos at a party, and Hans Ulrich Obrist saw it and recommended

me for the Istanbul Biennial curated by the Japanese curator Yuko Hasegawa.

McKenley
Why did he like the video, do you recall?

Andric
I think he thought the video made a lot of sense, because the biennial was, I think, about the war and discrimination among communities or something like that.

McKenley
So are those some of the ideas you were dealing with in your work?

Andric
I guess. I really hadn't thought about them that way, but when they explained it to me it made sense . . . I didn't really know the art world then. (*His cell phone rings.*) If you will excuse me. I am expecting a very important call. (*Andric steps out of the room. McKenley looks outraged.*) Hello? Hi. Yes. No, it's OK. Yes . . . I am here.

McKenley
This, to me, exemplifies—and I don't mean to put Josko on the spot—but again, it represents to me how the art world is run by fashion, meaning fashionable issues. I think an artist is more and more just an actor, and a curator is a director of a play in which his appointed actors just recite exactly what he wants them to say.

Morgan
What do you mean? I don't understand.

McKenley
I mean, art today is about what looks good and the context it came from. Come on, this video is not about anything, really; who cares what the images are like. What matters about this video is that it was made by a kid from war-ravaged Bosnia and that it seems

to have a "story" behind it, like it is about violence in Northern Ireland or whatever. But I think all these things are perfectly replaceable items, like clothes the curator is putting on the artist as if he were a model.

Ortiz de Montellano
I really think that idea is totally ridiculous, and it's really disrespectful toward the artist. And he is really respected in the art world. I mean . . . perhaps you are not aware of how critically acclaimed—

Morgan
(*Interrupting*) Well, I think she may have a point to a certain extent. Artists are looking toward opportunity. The art world fluctuates in terms of interest in certain issues, and I think artists consciously or unconsciously try to satisfy those interests by creating artworks about those issues. But the way those issues become fashionable is a complex process that I think is also influenced by artists.

McKenley
I am sorry to say that that accommodating attitude is true not only of the artists, but of those who write about art and who specialize in developing made-to-order theoretical justifications for a particular kind of art or cause. I think this whole phenomenon of the glorification of certain artists happens thanks to the fact that there are also social-climbing intellectuals who are willing to create a whole conceptual explanation as long as they get paid.

Morgan
I am sorry, I don't know who you are referring to, but I just want to say that that is not my habit, if that is what you are suggesting.

(*Andric returns*)

Andric
I am very sorry. Did I miss anything?

Helguera
Perhaps this is a good moment to bring up the next chart: the Hermetic Lounge poll data suggests that 88 percent of the art world feels that it is run by the rich. If this is indeed true—and you may want to contradict that fact—but if this idea is indeed true, what does it mean in terms of what becomes relevant in art discourse today?

Ortiz de Montellano
I just want to say that making a living from art is just reality. I just don't understand those who claim that art should be something like a religion where one has to suffer, like the old romantic notion of the starving artist. So of course money has to be involved in the art process; how would we survive otherwise? And the other thing is that if the rich do control the art world, I mean, don't they control the world in general anyway? It is not true of art exclusively. And that doesn't mean that those who have money don't necessarily support it in a sophisticated way.

McKenley
But that understanding is based on the imaginary notion that there is only one art world. I firmly believe that there is more than one art world, fortunately. There is the art world of the rich, which is a really weird place to me, like this place where people satisfy their repressed fantasies, be it sexual or desire for adventure or whatever.

Andric
(*A little exasperated*) But art is about experiencing other worlds! Why would you want to experience exactly the same thing you experience every day, the boring everyday life? You don't have to go to a gallery for that.

McKenley
What I'm trying to say is that there is a larger mission for art, that there are more important things to say, that there is art that truly says a lot more about the complexity of our lives and the

contradictions that we all live. I just think that we have constructed a world where we think we are free but we really aren't—the purported freedom of artmaking today is constrained by an economic framework. I believe that not everyone feels that way, and many artists produce outside of the art market, and perhaps that kind of art is not very well known, but it is freer and does not seek the fashionable recognition of the art magazines and the establishment.

Ortiz de Montellano
Don't you want to be recognized in the art world?

McKenley
Excuse me?

Ortiz de Montellano
I asked: Don't you want to be recognized in the art world?

McKenley
Well . . . I don't know . . . I suppose we all want something like that.

Ortiz de Montellano
OK, but would you say you want to? And do you feel you haven't been?

McKenley
Yes, I think at some point I wanted to be recognized . . . But like everyone—

Morgan
(*Interrupting*) Didn't you make art at some point?

McKenley
Yes, I actually started as an artist. But why? Where are you going with this?

Morgan
Why did you stop making art?

McKenley
I don't know . . . It wasn't for me . . . I felt I needed to move on.

Morgan
A lot of artists who were not successful in the gallery art market have moved on to become art activists.

McKenley
What are you suggesting? Didn't you want to be a writer in the first place? I recall that you wrote a book of poetry a few years ago that didn't sell. Did you intend to be a poet, originally?

Morgan
I am still a poet.

McKenley
So how come you are always introduced in panels as an art critic? Nobody knows you write poetry.

Helguera
I think we're getting off the subject here, and I think this discussion is getting too focused on the wrong things.

Audience member 1
I am really amazed by this discussion. I mean, all your views about contemporary art are so biased. I was hoping that there would be a bit more objectivity in what everyone is saying. This whole discussion is like a series of personal attacks between the panelists, and I just don't get where the whole point is in the debate . . . and if there could be a few more positive comments . . . ?

(*McKenley starts to look as if she were on the verge of tears.*)

Helguera
I think you're right, and perhaps I should apologize for not keeping the discussion more on target. I think we should go back to discussing the relevance of art in politics and whether you consider that art can contribute in a more relevant way in today's political climate. Holly, are you OK?

McKenley
I'm sorry. This whole discussion has been a bit difficult for me. I think a lot of what has been mentioned here has been inconsiderate . . . but I do think that there is a truth that we are not really talking about. Brian, you and I have known each other for many years, and you perhaps will understand more than anyone else what I am about to say.

I think we all operate based on the wrong reasons. I think there is profound disillusionment in the art world. It is like this to me. I think I wanted to be a recognized artist, but I didn't have the social savoir-faire, and perhaps I wasn't much of a good artist anyway. I often wonder, how many people like me are out there, in the art world, feeling profoundly alone, feeling that no matter what they do, it will never have an impact . . . When did the art world become a place where appearances are more important than ideas?

Helguera
Perhaps it is that we all love to complain about the art world, and yet we actively contribute to its continuation as it is.

McKenley
Brian, you are a ubiquitous and successful critic, but I often wonder whether you feel fulfilled by it. Do you?

Morgan
(*Embarrassed*) I don't know why you are asking that question.

McKenley
Look at Michael Kimmelman, unable to be a successful concert pianist, forever stuck, unable to get over the fact that he is the most

important art critic, but never what he most wanted to be, a pianist. Isn't that a curse, Brian, isn't that exactly what you feel?

(*Morgan looks at the floor.*)

We live in this play called "art world," and we are perfectly aware of its fiction, we know it is not about real life . . . We have made it into a profession to create an environment that others can partake in, but ultimately it's a self-congratulatory club. I fully admit that I have played my part, and it has been the one of a disillusioned activist, I guess the angry feminist. Patricia, we all know that you have a romantic relationship with Josko, and I totally understand your desire to defend his work, even to support him in instances where it could have been a conflict of interests.

(*Ortiz de Montellano makes an expression of disbelief; Josko looks embarrassed.*)

We are all human—but why can't that humanity really appear in the way we all interact in the art world? Why can't we just be ourselves and express our innermost feelings? I know most people may not feel this way, but perhaps there is something out there that we all have forgotten about.

Morgan

(*Still looking at the floor*) I do regret a lot of things that I have said, a lot of things I have written. I do think I have been a sort of conceptual mercenary. I have adjusted my views and stretched in ways that I now find a bit embarrassing in the course of my career. To what avail? I don't know. You're right, Holly, I did want to be a poet.

(*Recovering his old self*) I do think, however, that fortunately for all of us, the art world is separate from the act of making art. Art, I think, for all the poison there may be in the art world, will always remain a separate thing that very often is the result of spontaneous and real feelings. It may be made inside or outside the place we consider the "art world," but I know it is real and it is there, behind all the positioning and all the theater that is put in front of it. And one day we may all be gone, but hopefully the art will stay, and perhaps that will be the one thing that may redeem us as a society. I often wonder how we'll be seen fifty years, a hundred years from now—what kinds of things that we said or wrote will actually matter? And I think that for all the acting we do for each other, there is always an element of this feeling motivating all of us, and we should always keep it in mind.

Ortiz de Montellano
I don't know what to say . . . I think this is becoming too much of a talk show. We are here not to discuss feelings but ideas.

McKenley
But don't you feel pressure to act in a particular way in your current position?

Ortiz de Montellano
I don't know . . .

McKenley
Do you or don't you?

Ortiz de Montellano
(*After a silence*) Yes, maybe.

McKenley
Do you feel that you can't be yourself?

Ortiz de Montellano
Myself?

McKenley
That you perhaps are willing to sacrifice your real beliefs in exchange for those that you think or know will be favored by the powerful?

Ortiz de Montellano
I don't know which my true beliefs . . . are.

Being a curator and a dealer was a discovery for me. I did not know what my place was in the world. Suddenly, I found a place where I received attention, a lot of attention, for doing things that I didn't have a particularly strong opinion about, like Conceptual art. I guess I had an intuition about what things I could do that would be attractive to others, a sense of how I could make them desirable to others. And I really have enjoyed the attention.

But I have thought sometimes that this attention is totally artificial. I think that if tomorrow I was not running the collection of a very powerful and rich collector as I am doing right now, all this attention would dissipate. People call me from all over the world to attend openings, parties. My social calendar is full with international activities. When that started happening, my self-esteem went all the way up. Sometimes I have asked myself whether I should take it seriously or not. I don't want to give it up—I sometimes feel I am willing to do and say anything it takes not to lose it, because after all, it is business. And then there are those who want to see me fail, and it is that feeling that makes me even stronger, because I want to show them that I will not fail. Art is business to me: what stocks or real estate are for others. I cannot look at it in a sentimental way. It's not what one should do, not if you need to be a player like I am, not if you want to reach the top.

Andric
Patricia, I am amazed. I never thought you could think about art in those terms. It makes me think that for you the artist is nothing but just another quantity.

Ortiz de Montellano
I don't think you understand. I—

Andric

(*Interrupting*) Let me finish. I mean, I am not naive, I know that a lot of what we do is a game, but I do want to think of myself as important in people's lives. I don't know how to explain. I mean, I never wanted to be an artist. It never even crossed my mind. And all of a sudden I had some powerful curator telling me, you are an artist, or, this is art and I will make it so by showing it at the Pompidou. I thought, cool—I didn't even have a plan for my life. I thought I would just be a model or something. A year afterward, after making this video that I didn't even think was art, before I knew it I was flying all over the world showing it at international biennials, shaking hands with all these important people, and feeling the pressure from galleries and collectors who wanted copies of this piece. At first I couldn't even understand what this was about. Later I came to like it very much—who wouldn't? Who wouldn't like to be considered a great artist, a prophet, a visionary? Who wouldn't like to be important? So I learned what others said about me; I started repeating to others the reason why this work was important. Those were the rules, that's how it went, I thought. As an artist I just make things, and others explain them. But I have also thought all the time, what does it make me? Is it really me who people are admiring, or is it their own romantic projections about an exotic world, am I just, how they say it . . .

Morgan

A signifier.

Andric

Yes—a signifier for an idea that people want materialized in the form of an artist, of a prophet or something. Am I also an actor, a creation of some curator, a fantasy dream that someone came up with? And do I even need to know for sure? Shouldn't I just enjoy it and that's it, isn't that the way the world is constructed today? I may only last in the collective imagination for a short time, and perhaps later move on, like a temporary rock star. And maybe I do make people happy, continuing the myth of who they think I am. But it does bother me to be considered just a product, some sort of commodity.

Ortiz de Montellano
Josko . . . Were those socks really from dead soldiers?

Andric
Well, no. But that's what I mean . . . The public, the collectors, the curators, they only want a good story. It doesn't really matter what they really are.

Ortiz de Montellano
What do you mean? I did believe it! That changes everything for me.

Andric
You choose what you want to believe. As I understand it, art is not about truth. We project onto art what we most desire, I think . . . and I feel like a mirror, reflecting what people want to see in themselves.

Audience member 2
I am so confounded with this whole discussion. I am wondering whether this whole event is a performance or an actual panel discussion.

Morgan
I guess I am wondering that myself. I think the question is difficult to answer. As discussed here, do we really know when we are acting and when we are being real? And, when we are acting, does the discussion becomes less truthful than when we are being "ourselves"?

Helguera
Perhaps we can look again at the numbers. The Hermetic Lounge poll indicates that 53 percent of those interviewed feel that people in the art world publicly support each other but secretly antagonize each other. Fifty percent feel uneasy about being "themselves." Twenty-five percent often pretend they know an artist they actually don't, for fear of being looked down upon. Nineteen percent confess that they keep their thoughts to themselves while attending an art

opening, and most importantly, a staggering 88 percent feel that people are not sincere when they socialize at an art opening. Does that lead us to any conclusions, do you think?

McKenley

I have never believed in polls. Our society is run by polls today; presidential elections are run by polls, policy is decided by polls. But polls are always manipulated, and, even if they weren't, it is not the quantities that command any sort of truth. What is truth anyway? I don't think we can conclude anything from these figures, nor do I think that one can discern where the art world should be headed. And finally, who the hell cares where the art world goes anyway? It's a selfish thought. It's like being a shareholder pondering on the future of the corporation. We should really, really be thinking about issues of more relevance, particularly in this day and age, than the psychological disfunctionalities of the art world.

Morgan

But perhaps we have moved toward further reflection about how we see ourselves both outside and inside the art world, what hopes and myths we project onto each other, and where the contradictions lie within this vision. In the meantime, we can discuss whether we are honest with ourselves in this introspective exercise. And maybe, perhaps, we can become free in our distrust of ourselves, knowing that we fool ourselves every day. Art is a way for people to fool themselves and enjoy themselves in the process.

William Kentridge said once, when we look at a hand-shadow puppet theater, and we see a hand making the shape of a dog, and we laugh, we are actually laughing at three things: at the form of the dog, at the way in which the hand is creating the fiction of a dog in front of our eyes, and, third, we laugh at ourselves, falling into the pleasure of our own disbelief.

Audience member 1

I don't know if this is relevant to this discussion, but I think that whatever our intentions and agenda, we all should all be excused for being part of this activity that we call "art," and, whether we are all actors or not, I think it is important to remember that ultimately we do contribute to making art exist, and that is something that cannot be bad. We may be self-delusional, but is that so bad? Can't we also enjoy ourselves in our self-delusions? I happen to be reading the play *Life Is a Dream*, by Calderón de la Barca, and I would like to ask you to read the last paragraph of it, which maybe describes a bit of what we go through today. The character realizes that he had been led to believe that he was living in a dream, while he had been awake all along. This realization liberates him but creates the suspicion that he still may be living within another dream. Knowing that he will never know for sure that what he is living is for-sure real, he decides that he simply has to enjoy the moment. If you can read, if you please . . . ?

(*Gives a book to Pablo.*)

Helguera
Thank you. And with that contribution, we shall end this session. Let's see: Calderón de la Barca writes, in his work *Life Is a Dream*,

> *What are you surprised of? What are you shocked about,*
> *If my dream indeed was my master*
> *And I am fearing in my anxieties*
> *That I shall awake and find myself*
> *Once again in my enclosed prison?*
> *And while that shall not be,*
> *To even dream it shall suffice;*
> *Because only that way I arrived to know*
> *That all of human bliss*
> *Ultimately goes to pass, as in a dream.*
> *And I wish today to enjoy it*
> *As long as it shall last,*
> *Asking for pardon for our faults*
> *As from noble hearts*
> *To them it is proper to forgive.*

Good evening to you all.

The Foreign Legion

(2005)

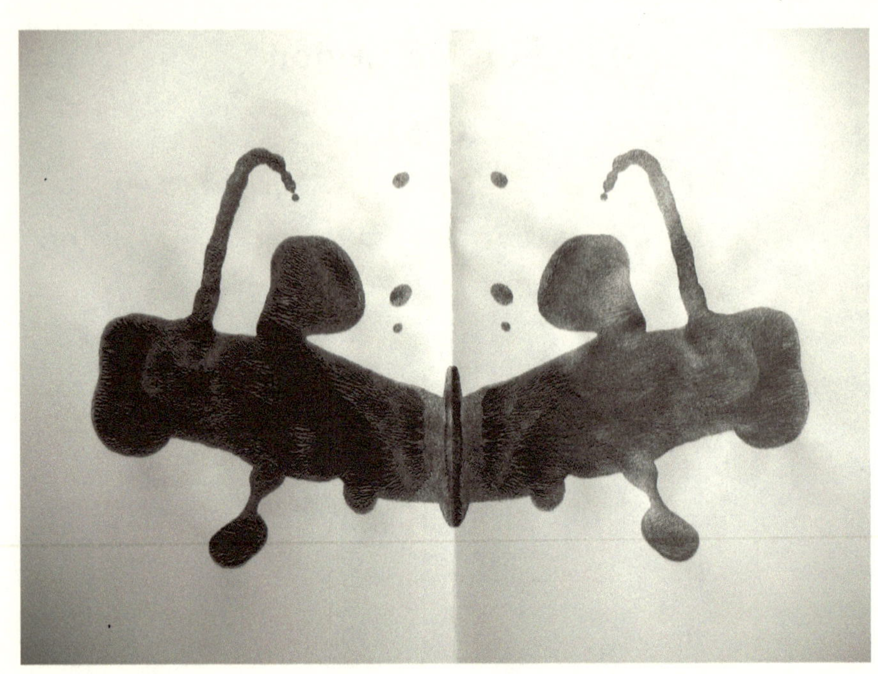

The Foreign Legion was presented on November 10, 2005, at 15 Nassau Street under the auspices of the Lower Manhattan Cultural Council and as part of Performa 05.

Appearing

Cardone the Magician, playing himself

Doodledee, art critic (puppet, played by Cardone)

Doodledoo, art critic (puppet, played by Cardone)

Pablo Helguera, playing himself as well as the role of **Doug Easter** within the opera

Thomas Keller, theologist (played by Filip Noterdaeme)

Elizabeth Levernier, philosopher and logician (played by Janis Astor Del Valle)

Dr. Ingrid Lipsky, psychologist (played by Stephanie Schmiderer)

Rhoda Pauley, opera commentator (played by Rhoda Pauley)

Dr. Robson Sawyer, psychologist/moderator (played by Kevin Scullin)

Tricia Sitwell, religious commentator/moderator (played by Susan Young)

Ghost of Susan Sontag (played by Cardone)

Swiss-German woman (voiceover) (played by Carin Kuoni)

Emily Wolper, soprano, playing herself as well as **Zoe** within the opera

Two panel-discussion tables are arranged on the right and left side of the space, and a center section—the main section—is set up for an opera recital, next to a few lounge chairs. There are also three projection screens, also distributed on the left, center, and right side of the audience. The action will take place in these three areas as well as in the back.

A Rorschach-test image comes up on the screen. A woman's voice is heard speaking Swiss German. A translation of her speech is projected on the screen.

Voiceover

Let's see . . . I see two women in the shape of fauns, galloping on top of each other, or maybe it's a single one beside a lake, and you see her reflection. She seems to be full of herself and kind of angry. She also looks like an extremely wealthy woman, like a woman of society. Her body is sort of disappearing at the end, maybe because she is running so fast, but maybe also because she is running away from her own disappearance. Or maybe she is trying to chase her own reflection. How many times do we chase our own reflection, like the dog that chases its tail? This woman seems to be very well dressed, but in an exaggerated manner—she must be *nouveau riche*. Perhaps she is angry because she can't fully escape from herself, I think. She is only half of something twice, and she will never be able to escape from her own image. I don't think she likes what she is seeing: despite the jewels she is wearing, she has turned into half an animal. Maybe that is the portrait of humanity today.

(*The screen shows Rorschach-test images.*)

(*Musical introduction.*)

(*Lights on Rhoda Pauley and Pablo Helguera, who are sitting on the main stage.*)

Rhoda Pauley

Good evening everybody, and welcome to tonight's presentation. We've just heard the introduction to the first act of *The Foreign Legion*. My name is Rhoda Pauley and I'm hosting this discussion with the singers in this new production. We will present highlights of the opera interspersed with dialogue with the performers. And we invite you to partake in our discussion too. We hope this format will give you a better understanding of both the artistic process and the players behind the performances we will hear tonight.

Tonight's opera centers on Doug Easter, a man who joins the legendary army of mercenaries known as the Foreign Legion. The soldiers of the Foreign Legion are famous for their anonymity: they are men without a past or a future. Once they join the Legion, they abandon the identities of their previous lives and pick a *nom de guerre*. It has long been said that those who join the Foreign Legion choose the mercenary life because they don't have anything else to live for.

With me now is Pablo Helguera, who sings the role of Doug Easter. Thank you so much, Pablo, for being with us tonight.

Pablo Helguera
Thank you Rhoda. I am glad to be here.

Pauley
Could you talk a bit about this character of yours, Doug Easter?

Helguera
Well . . . Doug Easter is a young, skeptical fellow for whom nothing really matters. Easter doesn't really have convictions of any kind. He is not a nationalist, nor do I think he is particularly religious, and he doesn't seem to find any meaning in his current life, nor in life in general. He is only full of hatred and willing to fight. So he decides to sign up and fight for other people's causes.

Pauley
Is he fearless then? Is he afraid of dying at all?

Helguera
Well, I don't think he's the suicidal type, but he is eager to go to extremes to find some sense of purpose. And he chooses to find meaning in the directive to kill the enemy, whoever that may turn out to be. In other words, he decides to enlist in the Foreign Legion because he is looking for an enemy.

Pauley
But the irony is, the enemy is nowhere to be found . . . right?

Helguera
Well yes, indeed. He is sent far away, somewhere in the African desert, to defend a region in the middle of nowhere. But then

years go by, and he never gets to face the enemy. Finally, on one particular expedition, he accidentally detaches from his garrison and gets lost in the desert. After days of wandering, Easter starts to see mirages and enters a hallucinatory mental state.

Pauley
And that is where the other characters of the story emerge.

Helguera
Yes, although the audience doesn't know it. In fact, practically the whole story unfolds within the mind of the character, but that is never quite explained to the audience. And stories unfold within stories, each one of them even less real.

He is living a series of visions, of multiple realities, let's say, some of which don't make any sense, some of which come to help him in his process of dying, basically. That's really what is going on, I think.

Pauley
He is an average man, caught between his search for survival and the incomprehensible reality in front of him. And that is the main framework of our story tonight.

I think we need to see a bit more of this multilayered reality onstage. What do you say, can we hear another excerpt from *The Foreign Legion*?

Helguera
Sounds good to me.

(*Lights go off on Pauley, and Helguera and Dr. Robson Sawyer are illuminated on the right side of the audience.*)

Dr. Robson Sawyer
Ladies and gentlemen, good evening and welcome to tonight's discussion. I am sure you are a bit surprised and perhaps puzzled by the unusual format of this evening's presentation. I think you will gradually grasp its intention as we proceed.

I am Dr. Robson Sawyer and I am your host tonight for the special public experiment and discussion The Foreign Legion: A Study beyond Rorschach, conducted by Dr. Ingrid Lipsky.

Every day we see and hear references to the work of Hermann Rorschach; the phrase "a Rorschach test" has become a commonplace way to describe situations that are hard to understand. Yet Rorschach's work remains fairly mysterious, including his famous inkblots. We are here to discuss them and provide information on Rorschach's life. But, most important, we will see them in a completely new light thanks to the innovative research Professor Lipsky will present to us tonight.

Dr. Lipsky holds a Ph.D. in psychology from the University of Chicago. She has written extensively on theories of perception and creativity, including the books *The Image beyond the Eye* and *Meaning and Perception*, and over the last few years her focus has been on the uses of the Rorschach methodology, which she will talk about tonight, along with the extraordinary discovery of some documents by Rorschach himself in the hospital library of the Mental Institute of Zurich. This is the subject of her latest book, *The Foreign Legion*. Without further ado, Dr. Ingrid Lipsky.

Dr. Ingrid Lipsky

Good evening, and thank you for coming. As many of you are likely not familiar with the field, I will provide a bit of background. Earlier tonight you saw a Rorschach test and heard the interpretation of one patient. We will be seeing a few of these throughout the night, and I will explain them to you, but before that I would like to introduce a few ideas.

(*Lipsky starts showing slides as she speaks. The first slide is an image of a Rorschach test.*)

We all are familiar, I believe, with Rorschach tests. However, there is a lot of misunderstanding about how they work and what they say about us. This confusion has led some psychologists to discard Rorschach as unscientific and his test as a simple, frivolous game of picture cards that do not uncover any meaningful

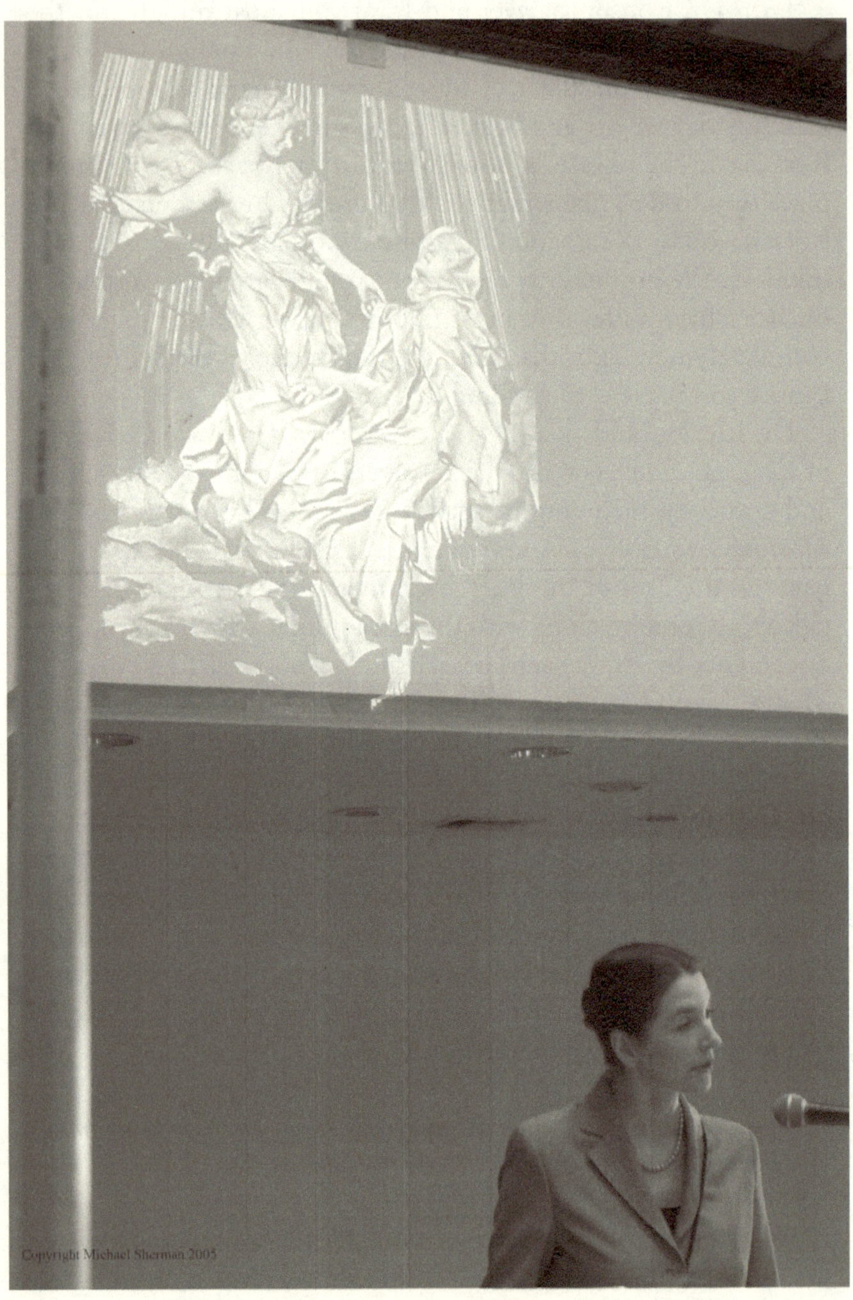
Copyright Michael Sherman 2005

information about a patient. This is partially because Rorschach's unorthodox methodology has rarely been fully understood. I hope my presentation will shed some light on the subject and help you appreciate his work.

The general belief is that Rorschach tests diagnose things like insanity, schizophrenia, or sexual disorders. While this is partially true, I am here to prove to you that Rorschach was onto something much larger than diagnostics and perhaps something larger than psychoanalysis per se. What I am going to reveal to you tonight has never been presented publicly. I hope you will share with me the excitement of these extraordinary findings.

But I first should tell you a few key facts about the life of Hermann Rorschach.

Tricia Sitwell

Ladies and gentlemen, thanks for coming. My name is Tricia Sitwell, and I will be moderating tonight's discussion, The Foreign Legion: Understanding Divine Apparitions. I appreciate your taking the time in this multisession conference to be part of this debate, which I am sure will provide us with plenty of food for thought.

We live today at a special time—a troubled time, perhaps, in which the subject of supernatural apparitions of a divine order is much discussed.

With us tonight to explore the phenomenon of divine apparitions and to enter into a debate about them are Elizabeth Levernier, a logician and philosopher, and Thomas Keller, a medium and specialist in divine phenomena. Mr. Keller is a member of the Foreign Legion, an international religious organization whose mission is to spread knowledge about divine apparitions and prove their significance as markers of the will of God. Ms. Levernier is working on a doctorate thesis about superstition and epistemic logic at the University of Cambridge.

It's great to have both of you with us today.

Elizabeth Levernier

Likewise.

Thomas Keller
Happy to be here.

Sitwell
Elizabeth: epistemic logic. What kind of logic is that?

Levernier
Epistemic logic is the branch of logic that deals with knowledge, more specifically, with what we call implicit knowledge—that which we believe we know.

Sitwell
Thomas, can you give the audience a general sense of the Foreign Legion's views on divine apparitions?

Keller
Well, as we all know, divine apparitions have been present throughout history. The Bible and the lives of saints give us extensive instances of them. I shall explain in this talk how divine apparitions give us a true indication of the afterlife. But I first should say that there are three kinds of visions, which I illustrate with the following images.

Just one minute while we put up the first slide . . .

(*In that awkward moment of "putting up the next slide," Lipsky, on the right side of the audience, puts on slide showing a portrait of Hermann Rorschach.*)

Lipsky
Rorschach was born in Zurich to an old Swiss family from the canton of Thurgau. He went to school in the small town of Schaffhausen, in an atmosphere of intellectual and cultural affluence. His father was a failed artist who provided a living for his family by working as a drawing teacher.

In secondary school Hermann's nickname was Klex, meaning "inkblot." There has been much speculation around the extraordinary coincidence of his nickname and the test for which he is now famous.

A game called Klecksography was commonly played by Swiss children at the time. They would make an inkblot on paper and then fold it so a butterfly or a bird would appear. Rorschach studied art, but he soon abandoned it to go to medical school in Zurich.

Keller

First we have corporeal visions, supernatural manifestations of an object to the eye. They occur in two ways: a real figure is perceived via the retina, or an agent superior to man produces a sensation in the eye similar to that caused by a real object. Corporeal vision requires a minimum level of miraculous intervention and is dependent on the invincible belief of the seer: for example, the visions experienced by Saint Bernadette at Lourdes.

Lipsky

At that time, in 1904, the courses of clinical and theoretical psychiatry Rorschach attended at the Burghölzli University clinic were taught by Karl Jung, who had just worked out the association test for exploring the unconscious mind.

In 1911 Rorschach experimented with inkblots and Jung's word-association test on school children and patients. But given his growing interest in psychoanalysis, he put aside the inkblots. He had become interested in the interpretation of artworks by psychotics and neurotics and their ability to paint.

Keller

One can have corporeal visions of the bodies of Christ and the Blessed Virgin, who are able to appear to men without leaving the abode of glory thanks to the phenomenon of multilocation. And, likewise, one can see corporeal apparitions of the unresurrected dead or of pure spirits.

Then we have imaginative vision. Imaginative vision is the representation of an object by imagination alone, without the help of the eyes. Sometimes the subject is aware that the object exists only in his imagination, but sometimes he projects it without being aware, as in supernatural hallucination. In supernatural imaginative vision, an agent superior to man acts directly either on the imagination itself or on certain forces calculated to stir the imagination.

Lipsky
Like many psychiatrists of his time, Rorschach was impressed by symbolic associations, and in a paper entitled *Taktgeber und Zeit* (Clock and time) he proposed that some neurotics' love of watches was related to a subconscious longing for the mother's breast, with the ticking representing heartbeats.

In Münsterlingen he started developing work in the area of reflexive hallucinations and developed the treatise *Über Reflexhalluzonationen und verwandte Erscheinungen* (on reflexive hallucinations and other phenomena).

Keller
The sign that these images come from God lies, apart from their particular vividness, in the lights and graces of sanctity that come with them and in the fact that the subject is powerless to define or fix the elements of the vision. Imaginative apparitions are usually short, because the human body is unable to endure them for a long time, due to their intensity. This kind of vision occurs most frequently during sleep; such were the dreams of Pharaoh and Nebuchadnezzar in Genesis 41 and Daniel 2.

Lipsky
Toward the end of 1915 Rorschach was appointed associate director of the asylum at Herisau, in the eastern part of Switzerland, close to the Austrian border. There, despite his busy job at the hospital, Rorschach found time to study psychoanalysis and psychopathology in religion. While investigating some strange Swiss religious sects, he examined a man called Binggeli, a leader of one of these sects.

Binggeli taught his disciples that his penis was sacred and that they should adore it; his urine was called "heaven's drops" or "heaven's balm" and he gave it to them as a medication or instead of wine for Holy Communion. One of his teachings was that the method of expelling demons from young women was for him to have sexual relations with them. Binggeli was imprisoned for incest with his daughter.

Keller

And, finally, we have intellectual visions. In an intellectual vision one perceives an object without a sensorial image. We think of abstract things on a regular basis without making mental pictures of them, and the same thing happens in an intellectual divine vision. An intellectual vision is supernatural when the object exceeds the natural range of our understanding: that is, when we feel we grasp the essence of the soul or the intimate nature of God and the Trinity. It can be prolonged for a long time: Saint Theresa, for instance, said it may last for more than a year.

Lipsky

Rorschach abruptly regained interest in the inkblot test when Szyman Hens published a doctoral thesis on such a test he had devised with Eugen Bleuler in 1917. Hens's technique was similar to Rorschach's of 1911—Hens had studied his subjects' fantasies using inkblot cards. Rorschach resumed his own experiments in 1918, now working frantically.

Keller

Finally, visions are not necessarily of a celestial order; visions that come from the Devil traditionally have been related to the overcoming of temptation. For example, Saint Anthony the Abbott and his visions in the desert.

Saint Anthony was born in the year 251, in Upper Egypt. Once, when at Mass, he heard the words, "If you would be perfect, go, sell what you have and give to the poor." He gave away all his possessions and retired into the desert.

Lipsky

In his test Rorschach used forty cards, fifteen of which were recurrent, and he collected results from 305 people, 117 of them non-patients, 188 of them schizophrenic. He showed them the cards and asked, "What might this be?" Their subjective responses enabled him to distinguish among his patients on the basis of perceptive abilities, intelligence, and emotional characteristics.

Rorschach developed ideas and patterns of thought that demonstrate an extraordinary degree of originality on his part. He considered the inkblot test a kind of mirror, the inkblots constituting optical stimuli that activate kinesthetic pictures in the individual that are then projected back onto the inkblots. It is based upon the human tendency to project interpretations and emotions onto ambiguous stimuli, in this case inkblots. From these keys, trained observers may pinpoint deeper personality traits and impulses.

Keller

To serve God more perfectly, Anthony locked himself in a ruin, building up the door so that none could enter. There, devils assaulted him furiously, appearing as various monsters and even wounding him severely; but his courage never failed, and he overcame them all by confidence in God and by the sign of the cross. One night, while Anthony was in his solitude, many devils scourged him so terribly that he almost died. A friend found him in this condition and carried him home. But when Anthony came to himself he persuaded his friend to take him back, in spite of his wounds, to the desert. Agonizing and weak, he defied the devils, saying, "I fear you not; you cannot separate me from the love of Christ." After more vain assaults the devils fled, and Christ appeared to Anthony in his glory.

Lipsky

His book *Psychodiagnostik* was printed in 1921. It is Rorschach's masterpiece, but the publication was a total disaster. The entire edition remained unsold, and those few who showed some interest were almost hostile in their criticism. The publisher, Bircher, went bankrupt shortly afterwards. Rorschach was somewhat depressed, but far from knocked out. In a lecture to the Swiss Psychoanalytic Society in February 1922, one month after the book's publication, he spoke of a further development of his test. But fate intervened. On

April 1, 1922, Hermann Rorschach was hospitalized after a week of abdominal pain, probably caused by a ruptured appendix. He died of peritonitis the following day, only thirty-seven years old.

But this is only the beginning of the story.

At the beginning of this presentation, you heard a recording of a Swiss woman, one of Hermann Rorschach's subjects, giving her interpretation of one of his famous inkblots. Let's move on to the next selection.

(*The space darkens and a video is projected on the front wall.*)

Voiceover

I see two conjoined twins. They are young and joined by two arms and a leg. They don't seem to be too happy about it. In fact, both are suffering and struggling to detach from each other. Furthermore, there seems to be a house next to each one of them. They seem to want to go in different directions, but each cancels out the other. On top there are two figures looking closely at them; it must be either of their gods. They seem very attentive to what is happening. They are not intervening, however. They are watching them kill each other. But they won't do anything about it. Do they want to see them destroy each other? Or are they powerless to do anything about it? Or perhaps both?

Levernier

I would like to comment on something. The story of Saint Anthony the Abbott purportedly shows that there are demonic, bad visions and celestial ones, and that if we hold on to our faith in Christ, we shall prevail. However, this presupposes that we are always able to differentiate good from evil through personal intuition. Based on this thinking, we could be having demonic visions for all we know. What if there were only one, evil God?

Sitwell

You concede that supernatural visions exist but that they are not divine but evil?

Levernier

No, what I'm trying to say is that it is impossible to prove the origin of these experiences on a spiritual level, and that furthermore it is impossible to classify them in any sort of moral order. It's like building a house out of thin air.

Zoe (Emily Wolper)

(*Singing*) I am only but an image of dust
A brief sigh of light
What you hear is only wind
Only wind
What you touch is your own touch
What you remember
is remembrance alone
Nothing is built upon nothing
like a theater of shadows
Well dressed of sweet, transparent nothing.
Well dressed of sweet, transparent nothing.

Pauley

That lovely aria from *The Foreign Legion* is sung by Zoe, one of the opera's main characters. Tonight she is interpreted by soprano Emily Wolper, who joins us here.

At this point in the story Easter has become fascinated by his own hallucinations. He has just encountered Zoe, who is a vision of his own making.

Emily, could you talk a bit about your take on Zoe's character?

Wolper

Sure. Zoe is but a figment of the imagination of Doug Easter, who, as we learn later in the opera, is dying and having a fantastic last dream. Zoe is like his alter ego, a very ethereal character. So as a singer I basically project myself, really, into Doug Easter, or rather into the perfect reflection that Easter would have of this most ideal dream.

Pauley

Zoe evolves throughout the opera, doesn't she?

Wolper
Yes, she does. She gradually becomes more real. And as her reality progresses, she gains a certain consciousness of her own, realizing that she is herself nothing but someone else's dream.

Pauley
Are you a romantic projection of his?

Wolper
I think it is more complicated than that. Zoe is some sort of ethereal, idealized being, and she doesn't necessarily embody love exclusively, but something else, like his spirit. She is the representation of a higher consciousness for this guy. Over the course of the opera, she becomes like the voice of reason.

Pauley
Possibly. But at the same time this feeling of completion never actualizes, mainly because Zoe is such a mysterious being. I think Zoe is the embodiment of the desert in the opera, the need to make sense of all that emptiness—physical and spiritual—that Easter feels.

Now let's look at the debate between the two characters. It's like a fight between faith and reason, with the paradox being that reason is given shape by faith.

Sitwell
Elizabeth, you were talking about visions and their foundation in faith. Can you elaborate?

Levernier
Perhaps it will be useful if I describe some logical fallacies we usually fall into when explaining supposedly supernatural or divine phenomena. The first one is called the *non causa pro causa* fallacy, or false-cause fallacy. This is when something is identified as the cause of an event when it has not actually been proved to be the cause. For example, if you were to say, "I took an aspirin and prayed to God, and my headache disappeared. So God cured me of the headache."

The second is called *petitio principii*, better known as begging the question. This fallacy comes into play when the premises are at least as questionable as the conclusion. Typically the premises of the argument implicitly assume the result the argument purports to prove, in a disguised form. For example, "The Bible is the word of God. The word of God cannot be doubted, and the Bible states that the Bible is true. Therefore the Bible must be true." Begging the question is similar to *circulus in demostrando*: the conclusion is exactly the same as the premise.

And finally we have anecdotal evidence, one of the simplest fallacies: to say, for example, that there is plenty of proof that God exists because many have seen him. It's quite valid to use personal experience to illustrate a point, but that doesn't prove anything to anyone. Your friend may say he saw Elvis in the supermarket, but those who haven't had the same experience will require more than your friend's anecdotal evidence to convince them.

My point in bringing up these logical descriptions is that the theory of visions that Thomas brings up is not founded on anything actually provable but rather on anecdotal references to the writings of saints that are improbable as facts. So while there may be religious interpretations of the visions we all have, they aren't proofs of any sort.

Sitwell
Thomas, what would you say to that?

Keller
I am not trying to show that God's existence is proof that we have visions, but the other way around. We have visions because God exists; they are a manifestation of God. Besides, I don't think anyone disagrees that visions exist, one way or another.

Secondly, logical reasoning is not an absolute law governing the universe. Many times in the past people have concluded that because something is logically impossible it must be impossible, period. It was also believed at one time that Euclidean geometry was a universal law; it is, after all, logically consistent. And we now know that the rules of Euclidean geometry are not universal.

The knowledge of God is attainable through the rational inferences provided by our visions. Even if they are inadequate and imperfect, they still may be as true and valid, as far as it goes, as any other piece of knowledge we possess.

Levernier

It is true that logic may not be an absolute law, but the conclusions drawn by it are intended to generate a justified understanding or questioning about the world we live in, not absolute truth for all. There is a difference between having a "feeling" that there is an absolute being up there in the clouds and creating a system that would help us organize our thoughts and our knowledge about the world. I don't see how, without logic, we could get any clear picture of our world. Subjective thought can take us everywhere and nowhere. If I dream that God is a dog, does that mean that I had a vision that proves that God exists and that he is a dog?

(*A Rorschach-test image comes up on the screen. A woman's voice is heard speaking Swiss German. A translation of her speech is projected on the screen.*)

Voiceover

This image looks to me like an open landscape. Actually, it looks like America, like those vast yellow prairies that you see in picture books about America. There are a lot of cows. It gives me a strange feeling . . . it is a sad image, as if it had been inhabited by someone who was very sad. But this image is also different—I think there is a landscape within a landscape, and there are people looking at the other landscape from this one. It's as if people had realized that an enormous window had opened in the sky, an invisible wall, and people in this yellow landscape had realized that there was another world within their world, something that they had never imagined. I also have the feeling that these American people are doing all they can to shut down that window.

Robson
Dr. Lipsky, can you talk about your book on Rorschach, *The Foreign Legion*? Why that title?

Lipsky
At the time of his death Hermann Rorschach was further exploring the relationship between perception and creativity, which as I mentioned earlier was always at the root of his interests. He had departed from the Jungian idea that perceptions are predetermined by the collective unconscious and that diagnostics can be based on that. The recordings that you have been listening to are from old films that Rorschach himself made; they were found recently at the mental hospital where he worked at the time of his death. They are very revealing, as you see, because they sound more like omens, like predictions, as if the viewer were only repeating words being dictated to her.

The point is that in his last experiments Rorschach was pointing to a new idea: that perception is not a prewritten code but rather something that we can write onto others. In other words: taken to its ultimate consequences, we can subliminally suggest ideas and influence thinking to others by exposing them to a series of images. His last experiments, which included these recordings of his subjects describing the images, dealt with this idea. The most important aspect of such a process is to make the viewer believe that he or she is in full control of the interpretive process.

Robson
But if that is true, how can we ever be sure that what we think—I mean, what we think about the things that we see—is not controlled by others?

Lipsky
According to these experiments, you can't. Paradoxically, you have only two choices: full skepticism about reality or full belief, with the hope that you may be right. This is the paradox that we all face as humans. Rorschach referred to it as the Foreign Legion theory: we all belong to a workforce, to a community, in which we

think we are free—but in reality we are simply obeying the orders of others, believing that they are the result of our own decisions. According to the Foreign Legion theory, mental convictions are like mercenary soldiers, under the guidance of external forces and unrelated interests.

Sitwell
Elizabeth, could you summarize?

Levernier
What I was going to say is that there is a fundamental problem in systematizing things that are nothing but ambiguous sensorial responses, to think of them as definitive signs. Our society has a tendency to mythologize and give credibility to things that are not even there or ideas that are altogether false, and I am sorry to say that religion is responsible for a lot of that—and, I would add, politics uses it as a tool to convince us of things that aren't true.

Keller
But simple logic cannot explain the complexity of our lives. William James wrote that we all have a tendency to find the unseen more real than what we perceive through our senses: religious belief is merely a particular expression of this tendency. He sees the power of religious belief in the same light: religion's abstract ideas seem more real to people and exert more power over them than everyday realities.

Levernier
But how can you possibly think that—

Keller
(*Interrupting*) In fact, it is natural for us all to think in terms of abstractions, of ideas we cannot visualize. We cannot conceive of goodness, beauty, justice, etc., as such, yet without the help of abstractions like these, we are unable to think about actual concrete realities.

Levernier

But saying that religious experience is more real than the real world is like saying that our dreams are more vivid than our real life.

Keller

It has nothing to do with dreaming or being awake but rather with being receptive to experiences that go beyond the traditional five senses.

Levernier

Well, I would say that—

Sitwell

(*Interrupting*) Elizabeth, do you mean that if something can't be smelled, or touched, or heard, then it doesn't exist?

Levernier

(*To Sitwell*) Well, if you let me comment . . . I was just about to explain . . .

Sitwell

Most definitely. But let me summarize first: we seem to have arrived at a dilemma on this very point. If our perception is not to be entirely trusted and if we operate at a simple scientific or logical level it would be at the expense of the sensorial intuitions that we develop as humans. And if we were to embrace pure belief, how can we be entirely sure that we are not mistaken? What is the ethical future of humanity?

(*Suddenly, Cardone emerges from the audience with two puppets.*)

Cardone

Good evening everyone, and welcome to *The Foreign Legion*, a special performance event for the Performa festival. My name is Cardone the Magician and I will be your moderator for the evening. This year the forum is formatted like a Greek choir. Instead of a general academic discussion, we will comment on the academic discussion or discussions called The Foreign Legion. In other words, this panel has been put together to give you, the audience, a chance to reflect on the work while it is being presented. Joining us, to help us sort out the issues, are two renowned art critics, Doodledee and Doodledoo.

There is a lot to talk about in this work. What are your thoughts so far?

Doodledoo
Well, I am very surprised. This is not what I was expecting to see!

To be honest, it is unsuccessful.

Cardone
Why unsuccessful?

Doodledoo
Because, because—I wish that it addressed the very serious issues we're grappling with today. This doesn't do it for me.

Cardone
What kind of issues?

Doodledoo
The issues we struggle with all the time! I am tired of ambiguous art. And I am tired of art that is obliquely political. Why be vague—why? Why not say things as they are? Let's be direct.

Cardone
How do you mean?

Doodledoo
I mean, what the hell is "The Foreign Legion"? Why not get real accounts from real soldiers about a real war? War is a serious issue.

Cardone
What do you think, Doodledee?

Doodledee
Well, I don't agree.

Cardone
You don't agree?

Doodledoo
You don't agree? You should.

Doodledee
No. Why should I?

Cardone
OK, why don't you agree?

Doodledee
Because I think that art *has* to be ambiguous, incomprehensible, just like that. Why spell out every single thing?

Doodledoo
I'm not saying be literal. I'm talking about two concepts: clarity of message and accountability.

Cardone
Those are big words.

Doodledoo
Well, I don't see them here. I hate art that skirts around issues. It's like saying, "This artist explores this," or "This artist analyzes that." But when you "explore" or "analyze" you aren't actually saying anything! You're only wasting people's time.

Doodledee
Sounds like you want "political specificity," which is the most boring thing in the world.

Doodledoo
Maybe politics are just boring to *you*!

Doodledee
Artists aren't journalists or cultural critics! They just show things for people to think about.

(*A Rorschach-test image comes up on the screen. A woman's voice is heard speaking Swiss German. A translation of her speech is projected on the screen.*)

Voiceover
I am seeing a man with a gigantic penis. Behind him is the horizon and the sun with two moons, which makes me think he is on a deserted island, or maybe in the desert. He seems to be surprised that his penis is so disproportionately large. What is interesting is that he is not looking at the landscape. In fact, he is turning his back to it. It also looks like his penis is continuing to grow, which seems to concern him. But wait . . . now I see something more. He seems to be hiding under a camel, or rather two camels. I think the man is carrying the camel on his back and crossing the desert. On top of it all, he doesn't seem to be crossing the desert horizontally, but vertically . . . is he descending to hell? At any rate, this man is doing a completely absurd task. Everything seems to be going against him: in a way, he not only has the camel on his back but also the sun and the desert mountains. It is almost as if he has everything wrong, as if someone told him to do something completely absurd and stupid, explaining it as if it were the most natural thing in the world, and he simply accepted it. So instead of taking advantage of that which can save his life, he is using it to kill himself.

Lipsky
As you hear in the patient's description, the image suggested to her by the therapist who displays it before her is one of self-recognition of failure. The subject was described as self-confident, but the simple use of the image has destroyed that very confidence and inserted doubt in her mind.

Robson
You mean to say that through the simple use of images, a certain conviction was subconsciously inserted into her mind?

Lipsky
Certainly. Which is not such a far-fetched idea if you look at the social history of propaganda and public relations. But through the abstract system you are able to introduce deep values, convictions, and emotional responses that would immediately override any logical proof or reason.

Cardone
Well, I think it's time to start a debate on a subject that is on all of our minds: can we speak about war art? Is it something useful, appropriate, and/or necessary?

Doodledee
War art is a waste of time and energy for various obvious reasons.

Cardone
OK, let's hear them.

Doodledoo
Yes, let's hear them!

Doodledee
First, we see all that suffering and injustice in the news, so we don't need to be lectured about it.

Cardone
But what about those who don't see the news?

Doodledee
Well, those who don't see the news are even *less* likely to go see art, so forget about them! Second, let's face it: nobody likes art with unpleasant images.

Cardone
Well, what do you think about that?

Doodledoo
That is absurd!!

Doodledee
Wait, I'm not done!

Cardone
OK, go ahead.

Doodledee
And third, art with a "social conscience" doesn't do *anything* to solve a problem.

Doodledoo
What?

Doodledee
Yes! It's better to go out and demonstrate or feed the poor or something. So I say: art should stay clear of issues like war.

Cardone
Doodledoo?

Doodledoo
Well, I completely disagree. First of all, you forget that a lot of awesome art was made during the war. Just think about World

War II! some of the best Picassos were made then, and also during the Spanish Civil War, like *Guernica.* And then the postwar boom that invented the art-world economy we still live off today! How do you like that?

Cardone
But what about the grim subject?

Doodledoo
But usually art doesn't really have a relevant theme, anyway. Like a few years ago in the art world, when we couldn't come up with any more subjects, there was this artist making work about the *muscle of his testicles*, creating a whole cult around his penis. War art is about something bigger, no pun intended, and it also stimulates the markets. It's making a true renaissance in art!!

Doodledee
You mean you prefer self-indulgent art about sex than opportunistic art about the war?

Doodledoo
You just don't listen, do you?

Doodledee
If I make a photograph about suffering victims of the war, I am creating an aesthetic representation that won't help the victims! It will only enhance my reputation and my finances. What would Susan Sontag say about that?

Cardone
Let's ask her. What does the spirit of Susan Sontag think?

(*A knock.*)

Ghost of Susan Sontag
What do you want?

Cardone
Is political art only an artistic representation of tragedy with no real social effect?

Ghost
I am against interpretation.

Doodledee
Anyway, the idea that sociopolitical art empowers people is total self-delusion.

Doodledoo
You're wrong.

Doodledee
You're like all those cynical art institutions, pretending that art changes the world.

Doodledoo
Art is our moral consciousness, we need it to say the things that remain unsaid in society. You're just afraid of seeing your own face in the mirror.

Doodledee
And you, you're afraid of accepting your bourgeois complicity in the atrocities that we all allow to happen.

Doodledoo
Me?

Doodledee
Yes, you . . . so you think its enough to go see art about the war?

Cardone
So what are you proposing, Doodledee?

Doodledee
(*Exasperated*) Let art be art!! What art needs to do is inspire us, to let us escape and live fully. Let's be corny! Send in the clowns! *Música*, maestro!

(*Opera music starts immediately.*)

Doug Easter (Helguera)
(*Singing*) A sweet
Old song
In this desert ground
Reminds me of what I have lost

Zoe (Wolper)
(*Singing*) A sweet
Old song
Will bring us back hope
And pave us the way as we regain our core

Easter (Helguera)
(*Singing*) The vast and yellow prairies, my house and my land,
In all their glowing glory they come all, to give me my sight,
The memory of my land spreads its arms in my weak grieving heart
And is to be regained if I wish to face my plight

Zoe (Wolper)
(*Singing*) An opening door to a new life,
Shall let us rise again,

Easter (Helguera) and Zoe (Wolper)
(*Singing*) We'll find
The way
Defeat every trial

Zoe (Wolper)
(*Singing*) To bring back our hope to a new life

Easter (Helguera)
(*Singing*) And to make this world shine

Zoe (Wolper)
(*Singing*) The everlasting bright light for the time of our peace and rebirth
we will ride through every wind and overcome every stride, and every foe
shadows shall fly
away from us
and light
shall rise
for all
seas of light, rise!

Easter (Helguera)
(*Singing*) Come forth
To meet
The light of joy.

At day
And night
Shining glory of our life
Shining glory of our life!

Levernier
I'm sorry, but there is something that needs to be clarified here. You can't base knowledge of something that is ambiguous at best with another ambiguity. You are building a ladder out of thin air. That's my problem with the time we live in now: we build our lives around false assumptions created by others or by the collective confusion of all.

Keller
But Elizabeth, may I ask you: What are you certain about? Isn't logic an escape for you?

Levernier
What do you mean?

Keller
I mean, don't you think that instead of clarifying things, logic introduces doubt into everything you do? Logic may help you doubt, but what kind of certainty does it give you, other than to prove that there is a way to doubt everything?

Levernier
But we can't live without doubt!

Keller
Doubt is rational paralysis, Elizabeth.

Sitwell
It becomes very clear in my mind now. It seems to me that Elizabeth is a person of faith, of faith in logic, that is, but faith nonetheless . . . Elizabeth, do you think that liberal minds are always paralyzed by doubt?

Levernier
Wait a minute. No! You two are wrong: there is no . . . logic doesn't . . .

Keller
It doesn't what?

Levernier
You can't just say I'm a person of faith, because that is the last thing I am.

Sitwell
But you are. And you may be as righteous as he is.

Pauley
I like this brief light moment in the opera, when there seems to be a glimmer of hope. It communicates the optimism that we all feel.

Robson
But how then can we operate at a logical level if, as you say, our logic is dominated by the emotional inclinations we've been trained to have?

Doodledoo
Your skepticism about change is unacceptable! Instead you propose to do *nothing* about the tragedies that unfold around you . . .

Pauley
At the same time it seems that Easter is in denial, don't you think?

Helguera
Well, I think his mind is trying to be optimistic. I think it is a natural human thing to do when we feel that we have been abandoned to our fate.

Keller
I disagree that it is an ethical dilemma. It isn't for me. It should be for you, the atheist, because there is no logic that could possibly explain those things that are deepest within you. Logic permeates the immediate reality I live in, and I accept it, but I embrace another logic that is based on faith, and that makes me freer than you.

Levernier
You may think that you are free, but you are trapped in your faith.

Keller
I am free because I am content and I have a God. You, Elizabeth, are trapped in your mind, and you are completely alone.

Lipsky
The moment we are born we become conditioned . . . I mean, we start a long and never-ending process of social conditioning that will determine our values and our interests. Who knows if we have the right ones? That is impossible to know, because in humanity there is no objectivity of values, only social conditioning.

Doodledee
I'm not saying we can't do anything. If you want to do something, go to war! Take sides.

Levernier
That is what you would like us to think!

Doodledoo
Do you think the soldiers that you send to fight are clear about what their beliefs are?

Levernier
How ironic that in order to be free we need to give away everything we have. How ironic that, because it is impossible to know the limits of science, because we don't know the answers to everything, we need to resort to a guy in the clouds who will solve our problems and take us to Heaven.

Doodledee
Either they are delusional or they are pragmatists who signed up to ensure themselves a future. We all do the same.

Lipsky
Our life is built around the conditioning of belief.

Doodledee
Aren't we all mercenaries after all?

Pauley
We all want a happy ending, right? Doug Easter is willing to lose himself in his mind to avoid accepting that happiness is an impossibility in his life. Ultimately, therefore, he is an idealist.

Levernier
How convenient to make people feel they are ultimately powerless, because that way no one will ever fight for change.

Doodledoo
You are just a pathological escapist!

Sitwell
So, in the end, Elizabeth, you "believe." Even your defense of logic is just a belief that logic works.

Doodledee
And you are a blind complainer!

Levernier
Well, but . . .

Keller
That's true. What do you actually believe in, Elizabeth?

Doodledoo
How so?

Robson
So is my belief right now that you are wrong just the result of my conditioning to believe that my mind cannot be controlled?

Doodledee
You are like a religious fundamentalist trying to change the world!

Helguera
You can't change the world.

Keller
The problem is that you don't have any concrete alternatives to a belief system. In fact, what do you believe, Elizabeth?

Lipsky
Yes.

Doodledoo
No!

Sitwell
Yes.

Doodledee
Yes!

Wolper
True.

Robson
Really?

Doodledoo
No!

Pauley
Perhaps.

Doodledee
Oh yes, no doubt.

Sitwell
Yes, what do you believe in?

Doodledoo
What the hell are you, then?

Levernier
I can't explain it in one phrase.

Lipsky
Absolutely.

Keller
Why?

Sitwell
Yes, why?

Robson
But why?

Levernier
I don't know! I don't know!

Doodledee
I don't know! I don't know!

Zoe (Wolper)
(*Singing*) Those eyes that carried you through life's pains
Bring nothing but a false hope of peace
Wishfully bind you to a ghost dream.

Easter (Helguera)
(*Singing*) If shadows are to fool my mind
I rather embrace their freezing gaze
Never wake again
To an empty landscape
rather die than kill the dream of life.

Zoe (Wolper)
(*Singing*) Nothing but a false hope
A ghostly dream
A vast legion of deceiving shadows.

Easter (Helguera)
(*Singing*) If these shadows lie
Within my mind
I don't want life
If shadows lie
I would rather die.

Zoe (Wolper)
(*Singing*) An army of lies
A pile of dust
A fleeting image of your dead hope
A pile of dust
A lying semblance of hope
Bound to a ghostly dream of hope.

Levernier
Perhaps I don't know anything else but distrust, but what else is there when there's no certainty anywhere? We are as ignorant when we know it all as when we know nothing.

Pauley
That was the final, moving duet from *The Foreign Legion*, before Easter's death scene. It is a farewell of sorts, in which Easter acknowledges his world is imaginary *and* chooses to remain in it. Somehow the false world he has literally conjured up is preferable to him than real life. Still, this leaves us with a paradoxical feeling of emptiness, maybe even futility, at the opera's end. Pablo, what are your thoughts on this?

Helguera
I think there is . . . It has to do with the fact that Easter never finds an enemy, or in fact, the fact that he is actually his own enemy. I think the true enemy is always inside ourselves.

Wolper
I think the ending comes without any moral, like without any message, as it usually happens in opera. Maybe the work is about

the absence of a moral. I think it's about perception . . . about how it is impossible to really know anything.

Levernier
I think the tricks of faith and our minds are things we shouldn't talk about with any certainty. Perhaps the lie is the belief that there is a final answer. You are right: I am alone, and, ultimately, I suppose I am a person of faith. It's an imperfect faith, because it creates more questions than it answers. But that is the way I understand things.

I feel empty and wrong, because I am not fooling myself into believing that I am fulfilled and right. So maybe it's not about finding truth but rather coming to terms with the fact that we may always be in search of it, like always trying to decode a puzzle.

Wolper
Sometimes . . . sometimes you look at the stars, right? And you are overwhelmed by that celestial immensity, by the fact that you are nothing in comparison, that you understand nothing. Who can explain the stars? I think to understand the stars you have to be mad . . . or an astronomer.

Cardone
Does any of this help us understand what we see?

Doodledee
I don't think so.

Doodledoo
And I agree.

Lipsky
The only thing you can do is sit there and try to understand. Try to read, to decipher, to see forms. But be aware that you may not be reading but only repeating the prescribed vision of others. The beauty of it all, however, is that every time anyone sees an inkblot, every single time, as long as we are humans with a living mind, we

will immediately see something in it—we will see many things in it. We will give it meaning. But you know what? Ultimately it's an inkblot. It's ink on a piece of paper. We are the meaning. The rest is only reference.

Robson

Thank you Ms. Lipsky. Thank you all for being part of this experiment. You all have been through a multiple-reality experiment, a Rorschachian performance that has brought you abstract people, images, and feelings.

(*All performers gather on the main stage.*)

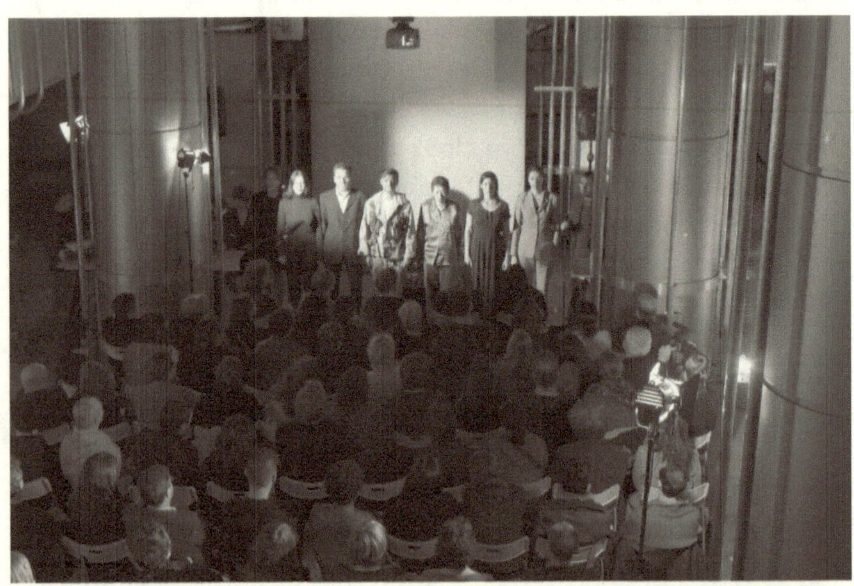

As you can see, what people see in images is mostly meaningless, has little psychological significance that we can salvage, and, overall, perhaps we have gone through a pointless task. But we can say that it has helped us to understand, first, that human capacity to see is severely limited these days, and, second, that our capacity to draw conclusions from what we see is even more limited. But as one of the characters said tonight, there is no choice for us but to continue looking. We all are spectators. Let's look at the last image.

(*A video is projected again onto the wall, with images of Wall Street.*)

Voiceover
This is the last one? I see a city, the downtown of a large city, a very old and a very young city at the same time. You can see the monument of one of their leaders, as everyone walks really fast to work, on a regular working day. Nobody looks at him. Everyone walks by looking at the floor. I guess they know him too well. Or maybe he has been forgotten. Or maybe they feel they have disappointed him, and they are embarrassed to look up at him. He looks very lonely up there, on his pedestal. Everyone is going to his or her business. I sense that all live with a profound uncertainty. Perhaps that is why they all are walking so fast. Perhaps no one wants to look up because they are afraid of the future. Perhaps this uncertainty about their lives makes them even more determined to walk the streets that way, to speed up their lives as if that gave them certainty. They are unconscious of this, perhaps; the whole city is unconscious. But what do I know, anyway? What are all these images, anyway? They are nothing but inkblots. That's what they are, really. They are nothing but inkblots. I should perhaps stop looking now.

(*Lights fade.*)

We All Are Streeter

(2006)

We All Are Streeter was performed at the Hyde Park Art Center, Chicago, on April 30, 2006, in celebration of the opening of its new facilities. The program was presented to the public as a real panel discussion.

Appearing
Pablo Helguera, lecturer
Sharon Stein, playing the fictional and eponymous **Sharon Stein**, Peoria artist and arts administrator
Encarnación Teruel, moderator, playing himself
Scott Vehill, playing the fictional and eponymous **Scott Vehill**, art critic from Peoria, Illinois

> *Loving Chicago is like loving a woman with a broken nose.*
> —Nelson Algren

Panelists and lecturer arrive. Pablo goes to a podium opposite a table set up for a panel discussion (he will show slides throughout the presentation). The panelists sit at the table. They do not acknowledge Pablo's presence (nor will they throughout the piece).

Encarnación Teruel
Ladies and gentlemen, thank you for coming to this discussion, presented in celebration of the reopening of the Hyde Park Art Center. My name is Encarnación Teruel and I am Director of Performing Arts at the Illinois Arts Council.

Pablo Helguera
Good evening, and thank you for coming. We will speak tonight about an obscure chapter in Chicago's history and, hopefully, shed some light on the link between the geography of a place and the idiosyncrasies it inspires.

Teruel

Tonight, in order to broaden our involvement with Illinois art, we present a debate around the subject How Do You Define the Spirit of Peorian Art?

Helguera

Oprah once said, "When in 1983 I set foot in this city, and just walking down the street, it was like roots, like the motherland. I knew I belonged here."

Teruel

Peoria is home to great and diverse creativity. Our objective tonight is to talk about its commonalities, about what defines Peorian art.

Helguera

But I am not here to speak about Oprah. I am here to speak to you about an almost-forgotten Chicago historical figure whose life has very much defined the city's landscape. He has been ridiculed and criticized as an eccentric, but he should be regarded as a visionary.

The history of Chicago changed forever on July 10, 1886, an unusually stormy day. An old boat crashed against the sandbar at the shore of Lake Michigan, 450 feet from Superior Street. The man in charge of this boat was Captain George Wellington Streeter, born in Flint, Michigan, in 1837.

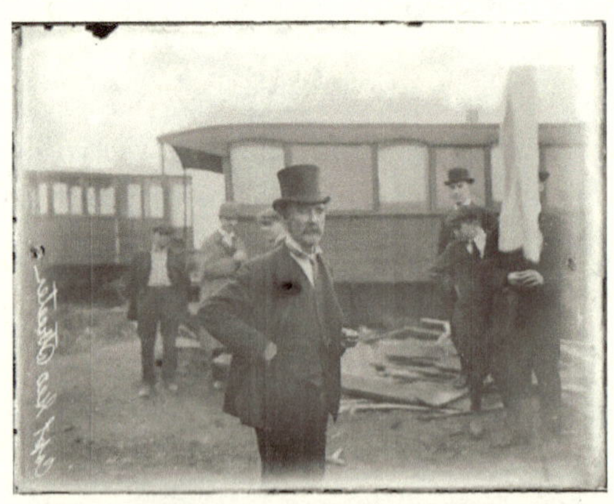

Streeter was quite an adventurer, and he had made the Great Lakes his working environment. He had worked as a logger and trapper in Canada, an ice-cutter in Saginaw Bay, and an iron and copper miner. He had joined the Civil War on the side of the Union and was discharged as a captain. Then his wife, Minnie, convinced him to start a circus, and he did so. However, Streeter was not an accomplished showman, and his enterprise collapsed into bankruptcy in two years. His wife left with all the remaining money. He started over again: he was remarried, to Maria Mulholland; and we don't know how, but the endlessly enterprising Streeter managed eventually to buy and repair an old boat, which he named *The Reutan* and used, we presume, for logging and transportation. After his accidental landing on Chicago's shore, Captain Streeter didn't have many options. He decided to stay in his boat, since there was no way to move it and he didn't have money to pay rent elsewhere.

Streeter landed in Chicago as the city was undergoing reconstruction after the Great Chicago Fire of 1871. He realized that building developers were looking for a place to dump debris, and he convinced them to do this near his boat for a fee.

In the meantime, Kellogg Fairbank, the New York millionaire who owned the land Streeter's boat was on, began trying to get rid of him. At first Fairbank had let Streeter stay where he was—he had seemed a harmless presence—but things started getting more complicated.

Teruel

With me is Sharon Stein, an artist who lives and works in Peoria. She is Director of We Are Peoria, an organization that promotes the arts in the city. We have also invited the international art critic Scott Vehill, also from Peoria and the editor of *New Art Peoria*. Scott has devoted many years to the study of artistic psychology and behavior and will, we hope, shed some light tonight on the idiosyncrasies of Peorian artists. Scott has contributed to *Artforum* and is very active in curatorial circles in the United States and abroad.

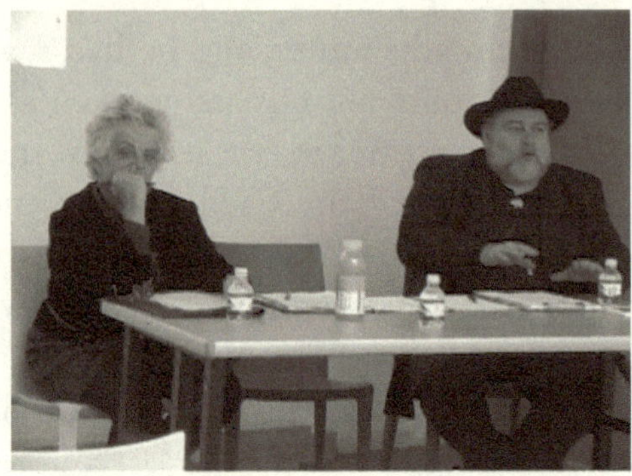

I'll start by asking you, Sharon, about the work of your organization. What kinds of programs do you do?

Sharon Stein
Thanks Encarnación. I am very happy to be here. We Are Peoria is a not-for-profit organization founded in 1977 to set the record straight regarding Peorian art and give it the importance it deserves. It supports Peorian artists and Peorian art institutions. We seek to prove that art made in Peoria is equal or superior to any art made in the United States today.

Scott Vehill
(*Smiling*) You know I am planning to contest that statement.

Stein
Oh, I bet you will.

Teruel
We'll get to that later. So, how is Peorian art better? I mean, how do you quantify that?

Stein
Well, it's very simple. Peorian artists are not dominated by the pressures of the market like they are in Chicago, nor are they victims of careerism and fashion or overshadowed by politics or rivalry. We focus on the work, not on the talk or the glamour. At We Are Peoria we seek to prove that the art of Peoria is balanced,

original, and independent, as good as or better than the art of any big city.

Teruel
What kind of programs do you do?

Stein
We have a lot of programs. We have the Peoria Only Art Initiative, which gives substantial grants to museums that collect only Peorian art—it is a very competitive grant.

Teruel
What are the application requirements?

Stein
Basically, the grant requires institutions to stop collecting art from places other than Peoria. We also have a grant for Peorian artists to make art about Peoria, the About Peoria Grant Initiative.

Teruel
Do you fund anything outside of Peoria?

Stein
Well, we do have our Make Me Peorian grant, which is directed to non-Peorian artists who might consider moving to their practice to Peoria. The grant supports the recipient for five years, during which he or she is not allowed to exhibit outside Peoria.

Teruel
And do you really enforce this rule?

Stein
Oh, yes, of course we do. Last year an artist we funded participated in a group show at the community library in Decatur. We took away the grant immediately. He tried to excuse himself by saying it was a very informal show, but this issue lies at the core of the mission of the organization, and we are serious about it. We can't

allow our artists to serve publics other than those we intend them to serve. We need to show the city and the state that we are serious about nurturing our arts community.

Teruel
I saw in the news recently that there is some debate regarding southern versus northern Peorian art. Could you talk a bit about that?

Stein
(*Reluctantly*) Well . . . it's not a very interesting issue, really.

Teruel
I think it would be useful to hear about it.

Vehill
Basically, some We Are Peoria committee members have been pushing for a South Peoria initiative, where South Peorian artists are funded to make artwork about South Peoria only.

Stein
Scott—it's not like that, how you describe it. It's not a real initiative. They are in the minority and they are totally disorganized and underfunded. It's not even worth talking about.

Vehill
But why not mention it? I think it's very telling. Of course, this doesn't sit well with North Peoria artists, nor with East Peoria artists, some of whom have already proposed an East Peoria Artists Council. And now a group of West Peoria artists have formed the West Peorian Association of Chicana-Asian—or is it the Latina-Asian?—the Chicana–Asian American Women Sculptors, that's it—and are soliciting funds from Springfield to build a museum by and for West Peorian Chicana–Asian American Women Sculptors.

Stein
That's not a serious proposal in the least! I don't know why you even bring it up.

Teruel
Going back to your grant initiatives: Don't you think that Peorian artists who exhibit internationally can give a good name to the city?

Stein
It doesn't work that way, you see. Artists who exhibit outside forget about Peoria the moment they leave. We have a serious talent exodus, and it started when local artists started showing outside. Then they wanted to move out. Artists who are talented think that by leaving Peoria and going to places like Chicago they'll have a better shot at success. The same goes for galleries. But it is not true. Peoria galleries that move out to Chicago inevitably fail.

Teruel
What do you do when a Peorian artist leaves Peoria for good?

Stein
(*Pained*) Oh yes, them. To be honest, I don't give much thought to them. It's their loss, really. Simply, my thinking is—out of sight, out of mind! They don't exist for me, really. (*Fake smile*) Yeah, really, it's their loss.

Helguera
The dumping and the natural erosion widened the shoreline, and Captain Streeter declared that the land where his boat stood was "a separate commonwealth, under the direct jurisdiction of the United States government." He declared it "the independent district of Lake Michigan," and began renting the land to whoever wanted to live there—mostly prostitutes and lowlifes. Soon it became a shantytown, and the wealthy people living nearby started complaining about the smell and the shacks that were lowering the value of their properties.

Teruel

I would like to focus more directly now on the main subject of tonight's discussion. How would you characterize Peorian art? How do you define its sensibility? Scott, perhaps you can shed some light on the subject for us.

Vehill

Hopefully. I have done some research on this subject and lectured about it recently in Austria. I published an article in the *American Association of Art Critics Journal* this year that touches on the character of the Peorian artist, as part of a paper about artists who live in cultural regions similar to Peoria. There is not enough time to present all the ideas in that paper, but I'll try to provide a summary.

It is very difficult to arrive at a unified theory of the Peorian artist's mind. There has been a lot written about it. Psychologists have been interested in it since the time of Hermann Rorschach, who in his early studies did research on art and madness. One of his subjects was from Peoria. Freudian psychologists believe that the creativity of Peorian artists is fundamentally rooted in a sentiment of abandonment or lack of external attention—very similar, that is, to the psychology of an orphan—manifested as something like a sense of inferiority to people in other urban areas.

Stein

(*Insulted*) That is just so absurd.

Vehill

I am sorry—we can discuss the idea later, but if you'll let me finish now . . .

Teruel

I'm sorry Sharon, if you could—

Stein

How can you possibly endorse a theory like that, based only on an insane guy who lived in the 1920s?

Vehill
If you let me finish presenting this idea, we can talk about it.

Teruel
OK.

Helguera
Streeter argued that the state of Illinois had no jurisdiction over shore land, based on the 1821 survey of the Chicago area authorized by Congress as part of a treaty with American Indians. Rather than giving the shore of Lake Michigan as a general eastern boundary, the surveyor John Wall minutely described the shoreline. Thus, when Robert Kinzie acquired a 103.27-acre tract north of the Chicago River, it had a definite eastern boundary. Over the years the courts had consistently ruled that the heirs of the Kinzie grant could never claim more than a total of 103.27 acres, and there lay the strength of Streeter's case.

Regardless, there were several attempts over the years to evict Streeter. The first one was in 1889, when five police officers tried to remove him from the property. They were faced by rifles and chased away. The second skirmish took place ten years later, in 1899, when five police officers managed to grab the Captain. His wife, Maria, attacked them with boiling water; Streeter managed to get hold of his rifle and chase them away. The Independent State of Lake Michigan was not going to give up its fight so easily.

Vehill
The theory is based on a study of city rivalries: Chicago is to Peoria what New York is to Chicago, what Istanbul is to Ankara, Berlin is to Munich, Paris is to Lyon, and so on. We see artists in these smaller cities exhibit a series of attitudes that can be related with Peorian art. One of them is known as "compensation for invisibility." The artist feels that he or she is not visible enough in the art world and tries to compensate by making work that is quantifiably different, either in size, erudition, or extravagance—the goal of these clearly intentional traits is to make the work more visible and emphasize its different character from

that of the centralized mainstream. An example is Bill Johnson's *Million Egg March* installation—he placed one million eggs on the floor and claimed it was a demonstration to defend the rights of caged chickens in an egg farm near Peoria. He thought one million would have greater impact than, say, a hundred—although someone told me the other day that there actually were only around nine hundred eggs there. But who would take the time to count them? Another example is the work of Archie Phillips, who is known for his famous performance *Explaining pictures to a dead Caterpillar*, which references the fact that Caterpillar trucks are manufactured in Peoria.

Stein
I think it is a very poignant piece.

Helguera
In the meantime, Fairbanks had sued Streeter for illegal occupation in 1893 and had won, which meant that, legally, Streeter had no right to stay. He did not leave, however, and continued to create schemes to prove that the land belonged to him. He even produced a document signed (he claimed) by President Grover Cleveland. While he never managed to get legal acknowledgement of his ownership of the land, Streeter continued to sell plots to other people, and the community started to grow. It went from Oak Street to St. Clair.

Chicago was changing furiously at the time, the fastest growing city in America. Another Chicago millionaire, Potter Palmer, realized that if he built a road along this new land, he could make a lot of money selling it back to the city. He started building what would be later named Lake Shore Drive, but he encountered the infamous Captain Streeter on his way. Streeter opposed the building of this road on "his" land, and Palmer died in 1902 without finishing his project. Legal battles continued between the Chicago millionaires and the penniless captain.

Vehill

My point is that life on the cultural and economic periphery leads to work that affirms a peripheral sensibility and thus to the eccentricity associated with Peorian art. This connects with something I call the "intense introspection" trait, rooted in romanticism, which creates the strangest obsessions. Another such trait is "negation of the outside": the belief that nothing outside of one's immediate surrounding really exists.

But my contention, actually, is that Peorian art doesn't really exist. When it is proclaimed a regional movement, it becomes a political strategy not an artistic one. Art is art, period. Regionalism is an expression of psychological weakness.

Stein

(*Irritated*) Oh my god. Okay, I really have to interject. I have never heard so much baloney in a panel discussion. I don't know how many more psychological definitions you have there, Scott, but I find the ones I've heard so far to be incredibly offensive to Peorian art and artists. First of all, Peorian artists don't suffer from those introspection sicknesses you describe. And it's just not true that Peorian artists are obsessed with Chicago or any other city. We simply don't care about them. In fact, We Are Peoria has an initiative entitled Boycott Chicago. As part of it, we prevent Peorian artists from exhibiting in Chicago or any other city and do all we can to prevent non-Peorian artists from exhibiting in Peoria, be they from Chicago or Kazakhstan.

Teruel

These policies seem a bit extreme.

Stein

Not in the least, if you consider that Peorian art has been so misrepresented by important Chicago museums over the years, and that the *Chicago Tribune* had the nerve to write in an obituary for Richard Pryor, a Peoria native, that the best thing that ever happened to him was getting out of Peoria. How dare they?

Teruel
Scott, don't you think that peripheralness is subjective?

Vehill
Excuse me, Encarnación—Sharon, if I may—and I am still not done—what you are saying all but proves the point in question, since you are confirming that Chicago art is such a sore subject in the Peorian art scene.

Stein
No—you are presenting it as an inferiority complex, and I find that completely insulting to Peorian art. Why do we always have to make everything about Chicago? Why?

Vehill
But if you have an initiative that is *specifically* about boycotting Chicago—

Stein
Well, we have no recourse, do we? Especially since there are people out there like you, saying that we feel inferior to Chicago. I think your way of thinking just reveals your own personal inferiority complex. You of all people, Scott!

Vehill
(*Sarcastically*) What do you mean, *me* of all people? I'm sorry, but you're the one with the inferiority complex, not me. You're the one who doesn't want to acknowledge the outside just because the outside doesn't acknowledge you.

Stein
Well, if that's true, how much more pathetic is it to be like you—you are totally ignored by the outside, and then you disregard your own city as revenge. Last time you contributed to *Artforum* was in 1981, and you pretend you have an international career? Give me a break!

Vehill
You're just jealous.

Stein
I don't sit around pontificating about other people's psychologies, pretending that I'm above the rest. I only value what I have. You disregard what's yours, and that's pitiful.

Vehill
How do you know that I disregard what I have?

Stein
When you're critical of everyone, when you think that everyone else is pathetic, when nothing is good enough for you, doesn't that say something about your psychology? I mean, ever since we co-curated the Peoria Invitational in 1987—

Vehill
I can't believe you're going to bring that up again.

Stein
Scott, you brought that awful German artist, who was the worst in the whole show, and you pushed and pushed to give him first prize just because you wanted to look international and because no one understood the work. And the Caterpillar piece by Archie Phillips did not even get an award.

Vehill
Well, yes, I thought it was a very derivative piece! And I still do. Even if Archie still won't talk to me.

Teruel
I think we need to backtrack here.

Vehill
(*To Stein*) You know, I can't believe you're telling me this. You know nothing about Conceptual art! You can't lock yourself in a room:

there's a whole world out there. People were furious that he won just because he wasn't from Peoria.

Stein
Well, you may know a lot, but are in total denial about yourself. How many shows have you curated internationally in the last ten years?

Vehill
I think this is just ludicrous . . . That is no way to judge what I do.

Stein
And yet, who's the person who bashes Peorian art more than anyone, and who, at the same time, every time there is an opportunity for someone to talk about Peorian art, is first in line? Look at yourself, you're sitting right here. The expert on Peorian art psychology telling us that Peorian art sucks, who hates Peorians and himself.

Helguera
Streeter's audacity reached a high point. He started claiming land owned by the Palmers as his own. Things escalated, and a decision was made to finally evict the Captain and his people. Streeter raised a small army; five hundred Chicago policemen surrounded the district; and the great battle for the independence of the State of Lake Michigan took place. Fifteen people died, and Streeter was captured and finally evicted. He continued fighting for his land in the courts until the day of his death.

The opening of the Michigan Avenue Bridge in 1920 catapulted Streeterville into the most prime real estate in Chicago. Undeveloped for decades because of the constant litigation, the land had been under dispute when the construction boom began.

Stein
(*Sadly, after a brief silence*) I dream of an art world that truly belongs to Peoria and makes it special. Meaning is always stripped from us, from what we actually own and are rightfully connected

to. When I walk down the streets of Peoria, I think about this. Why can people tell us how much what we have is worth? Peoria is our place, and even if it is not paradise we need to make art about that place.

Vehill
Just for the record, Sharon, at that 1987 Invitational—I know that German artist wasn't necessarily that good. But I wanted to set an example, I wanted to show that we can be international too. It's frustrating to remain local. I am a Peorian too, and I also want to claim something of my own that I can be proud of. I also want Peoria to be the center of the world.

Stein
(*Not listening to Vehill, almost in tears*) I'm from Ohio, actually. I went to art school in Cleveland. I always wanted to move to Chicago. And I did, when I was nineteen. It was an awful experience, living in a horrible neighborhood in a rickety apartment with mice. It was not welcoming at all. I've hated Chicago ever since. Peoria was not in the plan, but one day I landed there, I got a job there, and never left. Maybe there's something about that place that makes us never want to leave.

Excuse me, please.

(*Sharon exits.*)

Helguera
Streeter moved to a houseboat on the Calumet River in East Chicago, Indiana, with his third and last wife, Emma Lockwood.

Rumor has it that before he died he wrote a cryptic letter to the "subjects of the Independent State of Lake Michigan." According to some accounts, none to be trusted, the letter said,

> *Fellow citizens of our State: I shall soon leave your company, as the infirmities of age catch up with me. I sorely regret being unable to return your land to your rightful hands. God knows that I fought to the best of my abilities for our rights. But regardless of*

how many people try to strip us away from our lawful possession, and how many buildings may be imposed, the spirit of that site will always be ours, and the land shall carry our name, and our mark, for the ages to come.

George Wellington Streeter died on January 24, 1921. His body was sent back to Chicago, and hundreds of people went to pay their respects.

Streeter's land ran from Oak Street to the Chicago River and extended from Pine Street to Lake Michigan, in the place where Navy Pier, the Hancock Building, the Magnificent Mile, and the Drake Hotel now stand. Who would guess that the heart of this city was founded by this eccentric man, that it was once claimed as a separate state, and that the neighborhood would be named after the squatter and not the legal owner?

You may think that Streeter was insane, but maybe he was vindicated by his claims of ownership, of place. The place that he once claimed as his own, is now named after him—Streeterville—and not after those who purchased the land.

Identity lies between where we are and where we want to be. We create mental places out of physical places. We divide our territory, we plant whatever we like in it. We also can put a fence around it. Sometimes it doesn't really belong to us, but we seek ownership anyway, because ownership means identity. It is natural to claim something as your own. It affirms who you are. But remember—no piece of land is truly yours. That legacy is entirely in your mind and maybe carried along in the minds of others.

Teruel
Thank you so much for joining us. Next week we will address the subject What Is the Spirit of Chicago Art.

(*Teruel exits.*)

Helguera
Which makes me think that it's our stubborn embrace of a reality as our own that eventually lets us transcend ourselves. We all are

Streeter, because when we arrive into our lives we have no set place, and it is up to us to make it, which is a combination, perhaps, of a place in the world and a place in our minds. And Streeter, like an artist, made the place that once existed in his mind into the place that now exists in our lives.

(*Helguera exits.*)

Vehill

(S*lowly picking up his papers, meditative. He stands up and prepares to leave. He stops midway, looking back at the room.*) I really thought his work was good. You know, that German artist. I thought he was so much better than the Caterpillar.

(*Vehill starts walking toward the door but pauses briefly*)

I guess the Caterpillar was OK too.

(*He exits.*)

Manifest Destiny

(2008–9)

Manifest Destiny was first performed at the HAU Theater in Berlin, on January 19, 2008. Its final version, with three actors, was performed on January 27, 2009, at Cooper Union in New York. The setting is one screen with rotating slides, and a variety of selections of American and Mexican XIXth music, classical selections credited to pianist Joyce Hatto, and early twentieth century American music.

Speaker 1

In November 1839 American journalist John O'Sullivan published the following words in *The United States Democratic Review*:

> *The American people having derived their origin from many other nations, these facts demonstrate at once our disconnected position as regards any other nation; our national birth was the beginning of a new history, the formation and progress of an untried political system; we may confidently assume that our country is destined to be the great nation of futurity.*

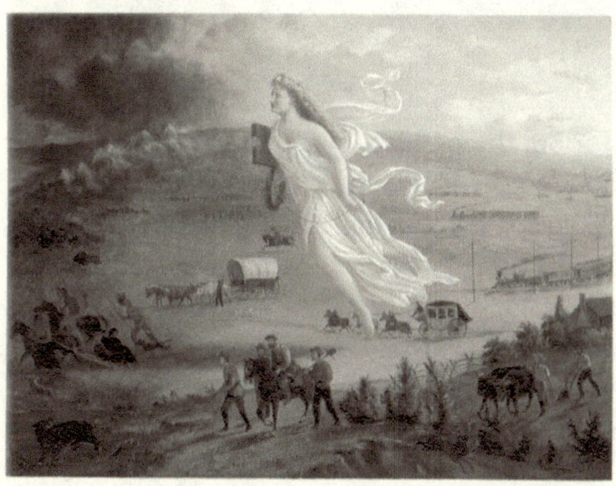

O'Sullivan's ideas provided the intellectual grounding for the notion of Manifest Destiny, a phrase that would have great traction among politicians who wanted to see the Jeffersonian dream of continental expansion realized. Advocates of Manifest Destiny believed that expansion was not only good but obvious ("manifest") and certain ("destiny").

One supporter of the idea was James Polk, a Jacksonian Democrat who became president in 1844. The United States was then a small country. Texas had not yet become part of the nation, the Oregon territories were not yet annexed, and to the Southwest the country ended with Missouri and Louisiana, which had been recently purchased from the French. Polk had a vision of expansion that would alter the history of the continent.

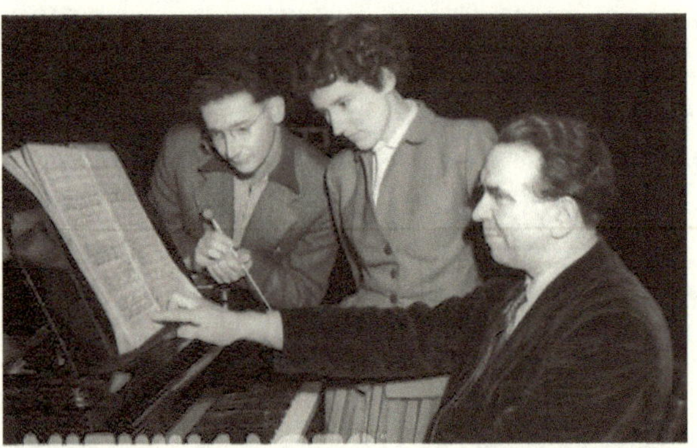

Speaker 2

On July 9, 2006, the pianist Joyce Hatto passed away in a placid countryside town in England. The next day newspapers around the world mourned her passing. The Guardian wrote, "Joyce Hatto, who has died at age 77, was one of the greatest pianists England has ever produced," and added, "Her legacy is a discography that in quantity, musical range and consistent quality has been equaled by few pianists in history." In the last years of her life she had gone from being a nearly unknown pianist to a superstar of the keyboard.

Most of her recordings date from the early 1990s, when she had reached an age at which many pianists have retired. Her production was breathtaking: it includes the complete solo works of Haydn, Mozart, Beethoven, Schubert, and Liszt, almost all of Chopin, all the Prokofiev Sonatas, and the complete concertos of Brahms, Saint-Saëns, and Rachmaninoff. She was one of just four pianists (and the only woman in her seventies) ever to have recorded all fifty-four of Chopin's Études, still considered to be the most difficult piano music ever written.

Born in 1928, Joyce Hatto was the daughter of a London antiques dealer. As a teenager, she said, she kept practicing during the war, hiding under the piano when the bombs were falling. Ms. Hatto made recordings from the 1950s until 1970—some Mozart and Rachmaninoff—but usually easier works. For the most part, she was considered a good pianist, but through those years she remained in the regional obscurity of a few local circles.

Her career was already in decline when she was diagnosed with cancer in the early 1970s. She retired to a village near Cambridge with a piano and her husband, a recording engineer named William "Barry" Barrington-Coupe.

What came afterward was to take the music world by surprise. Starting in 1989, Joyce Hatto began recording CDs for Concert Artist, a small record label run by her husband. She began with Liszt, went back to cover Bach and all of the Mozart sonatas, and continued with the complete Beethoven sonatas, then on to Schubert and Schumann, Chopin, and more Liszt. She played Messiaen. The complete Prokofiev sonatas were tossed off with incredible virtuosity. In total she recorded more than 120 CDs with impressive speed and accuracy; with her husband as producer, Hatto tackled a prodigious repertoire. It was an unprecedented undertaking for an older woman, made even stranger by the fact that the records were hardly promoted.

Joyce Hatto was something unheard of in the annals of classical music: a prodigy of old age—the ultimate of late bloomers, an unknown music master.

Speaker 3

In 1861 the United States was not yet one hundred years old. The Civil War had not yet taken place. It was the year of the birth of a man who would chronicle the past of this country and in that way become the most popular and biggest-selling artist in its history.

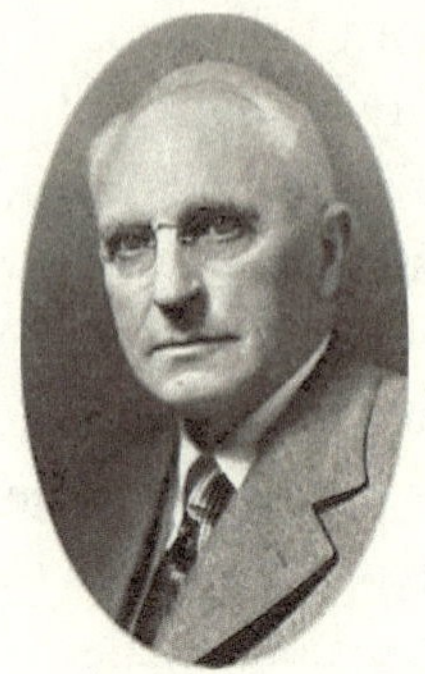

Wallace Nutting was born in Rockbottom, Massachusetts, on Sunday, November 17, 1861. He studied at Harvard and at the Hartford Theological Seminary, graduating from the former with the class of 1887. He became a minister, but because of poor health was forced to give up the pulpit at age forty-three. Like many men of his time, he developed a hobby of taking photographs, which were becoming more available commercially, and he was fond of taking trips through the countryside for this purpose.

Nutting's America was a country experiencing rapid change. The turn of the century had brought industrialization to the United States. Cities were transforming quickly, and people were leaving rural areas. Immigration from other parts of the world had increased, and the presence of newcomers was rapidly changing the landscape of America.

It was on one of his strolls in the countryside that Nutting had an epiphany. He stopped by a little creek, next to an old New England farm, and sat down under a tree with his camera. At that moment he felt a strange sense of nostalgia. "All these landscapes are fading away," he thought. "All this which is so truly American. I will save these images for the world." That was the beginning of an extraordinary journey. Without knowing it, Nutting became the first man to visualize the United States as a country with a history. With his photographs, he gave birth to the idea of Old America.

Speaker 1

The United States had expressed an interest in expelling the British Empire from North America. But when it failed to do that in both the American Revolutionary War and the War of 1812, Americans started fearing British expansion elsewhere in North America. This fear became a recurrent theme of Manifest Destiny and the main argument for the invasion of Mexico.

In 1836 the Republic of Texas declared independence from Mexico and later sought to join the United States as a new state. This was the ideal process of expansion advocated by figures ranging from Jefferson to O'Sullivan: newly democratic and independent states would request entry into the United States, rather than the United States extending its government over people who did not want it. The annexation of Texas was controversial, however, since it would add another slave state to the Union.

Before the election of 1844, Whig candidate Henry Clay and the presumed Democratic candidate, ex-president Martin Van Buren, both declared themselves opposed to the annexation of Texas. This led to Van Buren being dropped by the Democrats in favor of James Polk, who favored the annexation and went on to win the election.

Mexico had gained independence from Spain in 1821 and had inherited the territories of Alta California, New Mexico, and Texas. But the Mexican government was bankrupt and had a hard time governing the lands in the north, which were thousands of miles away from Mexico City.

After Polk was elected, Congress approved the annexation of Texas. Polk moved ahead to occupy a portion of Texas that was also claimed by Mexico, paving the way for the outbreak of the Mexican-American War on April 24, 1846. With American successes on the battlefield, by the summer of 1847 there were calls for the annexation of "All Mexico," particularly among Eastern Democrats, who argued that bringing Mexico into the Union was the best way to ensure future peace in the region.

This was a controversial proposition, mainly because the annexation of Mexico would mean extending American citizenship to millions of Mexicans. Senator John C. Calhoun of South Carolina was opposed to the annexation of Mexico for racial reasons. In a speech he said,

We have never dreamt of incorporating into our Union any but the Caucasian race—the free white race. To incorporate Mexico, would be the very first instance . . . of incorporating an Indian race; for more than half of the Mexicans are Indians, and the other is composed chiefly of mixed tribes. I protest against such a union as that! Ours, sir, is the Government of a white race. . . . It is a great mistake.

In 1845 President Polk sent diplomat John Slidell to Mexico City in an attempt to purchase Mexico's Alta California and Santa Fé de Nuevo México territories. Polk authorized Slidell to forgive the $4.5 million owed to American citizens for damages caused by the Mexican War of Independence and pay another $25 to $30 million in exchange for the two territories.

Speaker 3

"Everyone is badly educated," Wallace Nutting once wrote. "Most of what we ought to know is not taught."

Nutting became determined to record, revive, and preserve the best in old America, that which he saw was fading. He began to picture what he described as "America the beautiful," in and out of doors. He took up to twenty thousand pictures on platinotypes of typical countryside American scenes from different states.

In 1904 he opened the Wallace Nutting Art Prints Studio on East 23rd Street in New York. After a year he moved his business to a farm in Southbury, Connecticut. He called this place Nuttinghame. His hand-colored pictures soon became so sought after that he had to hire colorists to help him.

Nutting was inspired by the transcendentalist literature of his time, the writings of Thoreau, for example, that tried to recover the connection between man and nature. He saw his own work as a sort of spiritual restoration for the spirit of a country that he felt was fading away.

With the rise of industry in the United States, there was an increase in the variety and abundance of goods, there were department stores and mail-order catalogues. Nutting figured that he would take advantage of these advances to make his photographs available to everyone and through that process help restore the knowledge of the beauty of Old America.

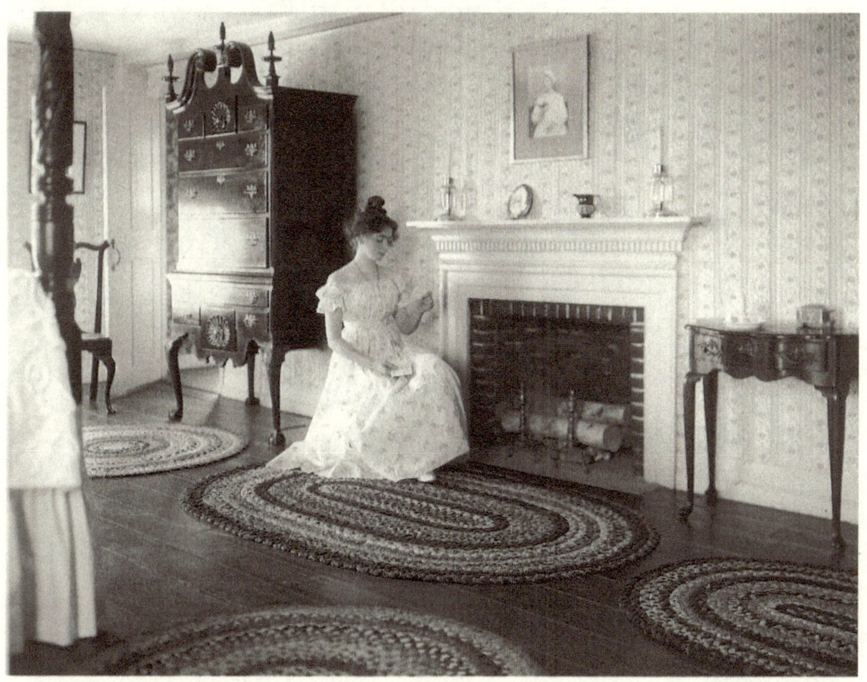

Speaker 1

On April 24, 1846, a two-thousand-strong Mexican cavalry detachment attacked a sixty-three-man American patrol that had been sent into the contested territory north of the Rio Grande and south of the Nueces River. A few survivors returned to Fort Brown. Polk's message to Congress on May 11, 1846, stated that Mexico had "invaded our territory and shed American blood upon the American soil." A joint session of Congress approved the declaration of war, with southern Democrats in strong support because they saw the annexation of Mexico as an opportunity to increase the number of slave states. Only a few voted against the measure, including Reps. Abraham Lincoln and John Quincy Adams.

Adams thought that the war with Mexico was another way for the southern states to expand slavery. "In the murder of Mexicans upon their own soil, or in robbing them of their country, I can take no part either now or here-after. The guilt of these crimes must rest on others. I will not participate in them," he said.

The United States declared war on Mexico on May 13, 1846. On January 9, 1847, they fought the Battle of La Mesa which resulted in the fall of California. But it was determined that war could not be won unless the United States army marched all the way to Mexico City.

Speaker 2

A few weeks after Hatto died, a participant in a Yahoo! music newsgroup posted the following message:

> *After hearing so much about Joyce Hatto, I started purchasing some of her recordings. While nothing I have heard is bad, I have noticed something eerie: that the pianist playing the Mozart sonatas cannot be the pianist playing Prokofiev or the pianist playing Albéniz. I have the distinct feeling of being the victim of some sort of hoax. Does anyone else share these feelings? What is actually known about the artist and the circumstances? I looked on the Web and all I can find is some sort of official story, nothing independent.*

Most of Hatto's recordings listed an obscure conductor, René Köhler, and the National Philharmonic-Symphony Orchestra, which didn't appear anywhere else.

A biography of Köhler, provided by Hatto's husband, eventually appeared online. It described Köhler as a Polish-French-German Jew, a survivor of Treblinka with the bad luck to spend twenty-five years in the Soviet Gulag—but there was no mention of him or the orchestra in any reference book. The conductor's bewildering biography only generated more questions. Was Köhler real? And if Köhler and the National Philharmonic-Symphony Orchestra were ghosts, then who was the conductor and the performers of those recordings?

A German music fan, Peter Lemken, tried to explore the matter further, making skeptical insinuations on the Internet. Lemken's suspicions about Hatto were based mostly on his incredulity at René

Köhler's biography. According to Hatto's husband, before the Second World War Köhler had studied music at Jagiellonian University, in Krakow. Then, the bio reads, "In the Polish capital, unable to join the Conservatoire because of his Jewish faith, he studied privately with the pianist Stanislaw Spinalski. In 1940 his left hand was crushed irreparably by a young German officer. He survived the Ghetto but in the summer of 1942 was deported to Treblinka."

Except that, as Lemken learned when he sent a query in early 2006 to Jagiellonian University, no record existed of a student named René Köhler. Furthermore, the university never had a music department. In a Usenet discussion, Lemken wrote, "What kind of frame of mind must one possess to invent a fake Holocaust-survivor biography?"

The final resolution of the Hatto mystery came when, a few weeks after Joyce Hatto's passing, Brian Ventura, a music fan in Mount Vernon, New York, slid one of Hatto's CDs into his computer. The piece was Liszt's *Transcendental Études.* The iTunes music library identified the recording as belonging to another performer, the Hungarian pianist László Simon. The reader brought this matter to the attention of Jed Distler, editor of *Gramophone* magazine. A further comparison of the recordings showed that they were identical.

At the same time, at the Centre for the History and Analysis of Recorded Music (CHARM), at the University of London, musicologists Nicholas Cook and Craig Sapp had been making a comparative study of performances of selected Chopin mazurkas, using software that depicted the similarities between recordings with colored graphics.

Although Cook and Sapp weren't familiar with Hatto, they included her in the study because she was among the few pianists who had recorded the complete mazurkas. They entered two tracks from her CD *Chopin: The Mazurkas* into their database. Digital analysis of the recordings was profoundly revealing: the Hatto version and a 1988 recording by Eugen Indjic, a Belgrade-born soloist, were identical. A Google search confirmed that both pianists were demonstrably real—Hatto had existed, and Indjic had recently played in Poland—which left the unavoidable implication that one was a plagiarist. The contextual evidence pointed unavoidably toward Hatto.

As Hatto's reputation collapsed, Barrington-Coupe did what he could to deny the scam. When confronted by James Inverne, another editor at *Gramophone*, he said he'd been warned that the magazine was working on a story and was aware of the László Simon duplication but couldn't explain the similarities. Since then, studies by professional sound analysts have confirmed that the entire Joyce Hatto oeuvre recorded after 1989 was stolen from the CDs of other pianists. It is a scandal unparalleled in the history of classical music.

Ms. Hatto usually stole from younger artists who were not household names. Her recording of Chopin mazurkas seems to be by Eugen Indjic; her interpretation of the extremely difficult transcriptions of Chopin studies by Leopold Godowsky are actually recordings by Carlo Grante and Marc-André Hamelin; her Messiaen recordings are by Paul S. Kim; her version of Bach's Goldberg Variations are at least in part by Pi-Hsien Chen; the complete Ravel piano music she released is by Roger Muraro. As reports come in, the rip-off list grows.

Speaker 3

Nutting turned his obsession with the American colonial past and the natural landscape of northern New England into a commercial enterprise. Despite his religious training, Nutting had a very strong business sense, and from very early on he copyrighted his images. As early as 1904 he started publishing catalogues of his photographs. He always wrote in third person: "Wallace Nutting's pictures had their origin in the love of an amateur for the beauties of our incomparable countryside." In 1908 he made another catalogue, and in 1910 and 1912 even larger catalogues appeared. This last catalogue had eight hundred pictures. At the height of his business, in the 1920s, he had two hundred colorists.

Speaker 2

Joyce Hatto's husband, Barry Barrington-Coupe, forcefully denied the accusations of plagiarism, saying that his wife's recordings were authentic. She was the "sole pianist on those recordings," he declared in an interview to *The Daily Telegraph*, and added that he was present "at all the important sessions" in his capacity as recording engineer. "If it was all a fake, why would I put my wife's name on it?" he added. "I would have put someone else, some Russian name, and we would have sold ten times as many. The English don't like success."

Barry's tone started changing after the *Daily Mail* dug up a 1966 conviction for tax fraud, for which he'd been fined and sentenced to a year in prison. At the time, the judge admonished him and four co-defendants, saying, "These were blatant and impertinent frauds, carried out rather clumsily, but such was your conceit that you thought yourselves smart enough to get away with it."

As his previous misdemeanors came to light, Barry gave a near-confession in a letter to the head of the Swedish label that had released László Simon's Liszt recording. He said something along the lines of "I did it for my wife"—as if they were both victims. He said he borrowed bits of other recordings to solve technical problems. According to Barry, Hatto had played all the pieces herself, but the recording had captured various involuntary grunting noises prompted by the pain from her advancing cancer. So he had searched for recordings by artists with similar styles and spliced patches into her work. "My wife was completely unaware that I did this," he wrote. "I simply let her hear . . . the finished editing that she thought was completely her own work."

As a matter of fact, Barry had actually been involved during the 1950s and 1960s in a type of musical scam that was common in England and America at the time. It consisted in stealing authentic recordings and re-releasing them under a new discount label with fictional names of interpreters and orchestras. The performers of such recordings, which sold for around a dollar apiece, had artful pseudonyms—Paul Procopolis, Giuseppe Parolini, the Cincinnati Pro Arte Philharmonic, the Munich Greater State Symphony—and Barry is credited with coining the wittiest of all: Wilhelm Havagesse (conducting the made-up Zurich Municipal Orchestra playing Rimsky-Korsakov's *Scheherazade*).

In order to make up for his wife's insufficient talent, Barry used his to concoct the perfect pianist, displaying her mastery in more than one hundred CDs, giving to the imagination a master for the ages.

Speaker 1

President Polk sent a second army, under General Winfield Scott, to the port of Veracruz by sea to begin an invasion of the Mexican heartland. A group of twelve thousand volunteer and regular soldiers successfully offloaded supplies, weapons, and horses near the walled city, which responded as best it could with its own artillery. The effect of the extended barrage destroyed the will of the Mexican side to fight against a numerically superior force, and they surrendered the city after twelve days under siege.

Scott then marched westward toward Mexico City with 8,500 troops, while general Santa Anna set up a defensive position in a canyon around the main road at the halfway mark to Mexico City, near the hamlet of Cerro Gordo. Due to strategic mistakes, however, Santa Anna and his troops were routed. The United States army suffered four hundred casualties, while the Mexicans suffered over a thousand deaths and three thousand taken prisoner.

In May, Mexico City was laid open in the Battle of Chapultepec and subsequently occupied. Winfield Scott became an American national hero after his victories in the Mexican-American War, and he later became military governor of occupied Mexico City.

The toll of the war was enormous for Mexico, which lost nearly half of its territory during that conflict. The Treaty of Guadalupe Hidalgo, signed on February 2, 1848, by American diplomat Nicholas Trist, ended the war and gave the United States undisputed control of Texas, established the U.S.–Mexican border of the Rio Grande River, and ceded to the United States the present-day states of California, Nevada, and Utah, and parts of Colorado, Arizona, New Mexico, and Wyoming. In return, Mexico received US $15,000,000—less than half the amount the United States had offered Mexico for the land before the opening of hostilities—and the U.S. agreed to assume $3.25 million in debt the Mexican government owed to American citizens. The acquisition was controversial at time, especially among those American politicians who had opposed the war from the start. A leading United States newspaper, the *Whig Intelligencer*, sardonically concluded, "We take nothing by conquest. . . . Thank God."

Congressman Abraham Lincoln attacked President Polk, saying that the war had been "unnecessarily and unconstitutionally begun by the President of the United States." Ralph Waldo Emerson rejected war "as a means of achieving America's destiny," although he added that "most of the great results of history are brought about by discreditable means." General Grant, who led the troops during the war, later said, "To this day I regard the war as one of the most unjust ever waged by a stronger against a weaker nation. I have always believed that it was on our part most unjust." Grant also expressed the view that the war against Mexico had brought God's punishment on the United States in the form of the American Civil War: "The Southern rebellion was largely the outgrowth of the Mexican war. Nations, like individuals, are punished for their transgressions. We got our punishment in the most sanguinary and expensive war of modern times."

Speaker 3

Wallace Nutting died in 1941. At the time of his death, he had built one of the most successful decorative-arts empires in the United States. According to his records, he had sold ten million original photographs, likely the highest figure ever reached by any artist, commercial or not, of any era. Today, many samples of "colonial furniture" that Nutting produced, which mostly were bogus fabrications of supposedly authentic historic styles, are now worth more than the actual pieces that truly belong to the colonial period.

But his impact went much beyond the commercial success. Nutting continued preaching morality through his images, turning the lens of the camera into his pulpit. He preached about an America that never existed, one that he wished had existed. His photography prescribed the traditional modes of behavior and decoration that built suburban America, spread distrust for the new immigrant, and invented a collective memory for a nation that was too young yet to have any. Nutting was the father of Americana, of that peculiar and prevailing romantic notion in the United

States that the national past is benevolent, that the development of America is a beautiful fairy-tale. His legacy is still felt in many successful businesses that cater to American suburban ideals of beauty. (*Screen shows an image of Martha Stewart magazine.*)

Speaker 2

After Hatto's death from cancer on June 29, 2006, at the age of seventy-seven, obituaries and tributes recycled the most striking superlatives ("as completely satisfying a pianist as anyone in the history of recorded music," "a national treasure"). Her funeral took place at a crematory in Cambridge, a secular ceremony organized by her husband. Mourners listened to music—Bach, Brahms, Chopin, Debussy—from a Hatto sampler CD issued by Concert Artist a few months earlier. Humility was the theme of Barry's prepared remarks, beginning with an apology to his wife that a service was being held in the first place, contrary to her wish to avoid a ceremony, "her final public appearance." As an artist and a teacher, he said, "she would say . . . there is God, the composer, and then you. Nothing comes between composer and the listener. With Joyce you will seek vainly for ostentation, no grand 'Hatto' moments, simply the music."

Speaker 1

O'Sullivan finished his 1839 article as follows:

> *This is our high destiny, and in nature's eternal, inevitable decree of cause and effect we must accomplish it. All this will be our future history, to establish on earth the moral dignity and salvation of man—the immutable truth and beneficence of God. For this blessed mission to the nations of the world, which are shut out from the life-giving light of truth, has America been chosen; and her high example shall smite unto death the tyranny of kings, hierarchs, and oligarchs, and carry the glad tidings of peace and good will where myriads now endure an existence scarcely more enviable than that of beasts of the field. Who, then, can doubt that our country is destined to be the great nation of futurity?*

Speaker 2
What is it about those images that we construct about ourselves, and the way that we go about taking over the world to promote them?

Speaker 3
Be it violent or benevolent, the virus of utopia has a way of infecting us with hopes and ideals that may be false, unfounded, and rooted in fantasy or denial, but their common denominator is that they appeal to something that we *want* to exist, to our unexpressed desires, helping us project a sugar-coated reality.

Speaker 1
We want them. Sometimes they bother us, or we are suspicious of them, but they are so tempting that we usually succumb to their attraction.

Speaker 2
And once we do, we become part of them, we become co-conspirators, enactors of their proposed fictions.

Speaker 3
We allow our world to be constructed with dubious means, but we try to justify it to ourselves because that is the way things are, because that is how things were before we arrived,

Speaker 1
and who are we to individually take on an entire system of deception? We are very small, and it is so overpowering.

Speaker 2
When we accept that, we also accept the divorce of cause and effect and past and present, and the fusion of right and wrong.

Speaker 3
That is how we are, full of contradictions, and it is perhaps our manifest destiny, as a society, to always fall in love with the latest fable,

Speaker 1
be deceived, and after we have been painfully hurt by our deception,

Speaker 2
eagerly await the next promising deception to take over and give us at least temporary relief,

Speaker 3
telling us a story that we desperately want to be true,

Speaker 1
but that we quietly know is too perfect to be true.

Bibliography

Brosterman, Norman, and Kiyoshi Togashi. *Inventing Kindergarten.* New York: H. N. Abrams, 1997.

Calhoun, John Caldwell. "John C. Calhoun's Senate speech against the annexation of Mexico, Jan. 4, 1848." In *The Works of John C. Calhoun,* edited by Richard K Crallé, vol. IV, 410–411. New York: Appleton and Company, 1853.

Denenberg, Thomas Andrew. *Wallace Nutting and the Invention of Old America.* New Haven, Conn., and London: Yale University Press, 2003.

Dixon, Daniel. "Florence Foster Jenkins: The Diva of Din." *Coronet,* December 1957.

Dutton, Denis. "Shoot the Piano Player." *New York Times,* February 26, 2007.

Lopez-Pumarejo, Tomas. "Telenovelas: a Global Product." In *Telenovela Institute: Los del Este/Eastenders,* edited by Pablo Helguera, 6–7. London: Routledge, 2004.

Schroeder, John H. *Mr. Polk's War: American Opposition and Dissent, 1846–1848.* Madison, Wis.: University of Wisconsin Press, 1973.

Singer, Mark. "Joyce Hatto: Notes on a Scandal." *Daily Telegraph,* November 10, 2007.

Spinoza, Benedict de. *Ethics.* Edited by James Gutman. New York: Hafner Publishing Company, 1949.

Vega, Lope de. "La Vida es sueño." In *El caballero de Olmedo,* by Lope de Vega, Rogelio Reyes Cano, Eva María Reyes Pérez, and Pedro Calderón de la Barca. Barcelona: Grupo Hermes Editora General, 1997.

Weschler, Lawrence. *Mr. Wilson's Cabinet of Wonder.* New York: Vintage Books, 1995.

Wheelan, Joseph. *Invading Mexico: America's Continental Dream and the Mexican War, 1846–1848.* New York: Carroll & Graf Publishers, 2007.

Yates, Frances. *The Art of Memory.* Chicago: University of Chicago Press, 1966.

About the Author

Pablo Helguera (Mexico City, 1971) is a visual and performance artist. His past projects include a phonographic archive of dying languages, a memory theater, and fourteen visual artist heteronyms and four fictional opera composers.

Helguera is the author of six books, including *The Pablo Helguera Manual of Contemporary Art Style* (2005, English version 2007), *The Witches of Tepoztlán* (*and Other Unpublished Operas*) (2007), the novel *The Boy Inside the Letter* (2008), and *Artoons* (2009). In 2006 he drove from Anchorage to Tierra del Fuego with a collapsible schoolhouse, organizing discussions, activist happenings, and civic ceremonies along the way (*The School of Panamerican Unrest*). He is Director of Adult and Academic Programs in the Department of Education at the Museum of Modern Art in New York and the recipient of a Guggenheim Fellowship in 2008. His play *The Juvenal Players* will be produced by Grand Arts in Kansas City, Missouri, in 2009.

He lives in Brooklyn with his wife, Dannielle Tegeder, and their cat, Ceniza.

Performance Chronology

1992
Echoes, School of the Art Institute of Chicago

1993
Los Dias Vacios, School of the Art Institute of Chicago

Babel, Gallery 2, School of the Art Institute of Chicago

1994
Circorama de la Nostalgia Operistica, Chicago Cultural Center

Polanco, public performance, Mexico City

1995
The Memory Palace of Matteo Ricci, Blue Rider Theater, Chicago

1996
The Palace (and Other Pilsen Ghost Stories), Blue Rider Theater, Chicago

1997
Juruá, Randolph Street Gallery, Chicago

1998
Binomio, Museo de Arte Moderno, Mexico City

2000
From the Vocal Archives of Florence Foster Jenkins, Ex-Teresa Espacio Alternativo, Mexico City; Matice Hrvatska Gallery, Zagreb, Croatia

Everythingness, Viper Festival Basel

2001
Mock Turtle, or An Epistemological Study of Mock Turtles and Their Relevance to the Origin of the Avant-Garde, Center for Paper and Book Arts, Columbia College, Chicago; University of Oregon, Portland

The Pablo Helguera Singing Telegram Show, The Brewster Project, Brewster, New York

2002
Theatrum Anatomicum (or How to Dissect a Melodrama); P.S.1 Contemporary Art Center, New York; IFA Galerie, Bonn; BAK, Utrecht

Eight American Folksongs, Sonnet Theater, New York

The Museum as Medium Symposium (organizer), Solomon R. Guggenheim Museum, New York; Centro Nacional de las Artes, Mexico City

2003
Parallel Lives, The Museum of Modern Art, New York

First Mexico City Congress of Urban Purification, Mexico City

2004
First Imaginary Forum of Mental Sculpture, Sculpture Center, New York

The Kingston Recital, Stanley Picker Gallery, Kingston University, London

Conservatory of Dead Languages, San Juan Poligraphic Triennial

The Symposium, PR04, Rincón, Puerto Rico

2005
The Foreign Legion, Lower Manhattan Cultural Council, Performa 05, New York

We All Need a Pygmalion, Banff Center, Banff, Canada

2006
We All Are Streeter, Hyde Park Art Center, Chicago

Panamerican Ceremonies of *The School of Panamerican Unrest* (various locations)

On Extinction, Center for Book Arts, New York

2007
The Witches of Tepoztlán (and Other Unpublished Operas), Enrique Guerrero Gallery, Mexico City

2008
Orizaba, Weatherspoon Museum, Greensboro, North Carolina

The Boy Inside the Letter, Queens Museum, New York; Casa del Lago, Mexico City

The Seven Bridges of Königsberg, Forever and Today, New York

2009
Revolver, Centro de Arte Reina Sofía, Madrid

The Juvenal Players, Grand Arts, Kansas City, Missouri; The Kitchen, New York (upcoming, 2010)

The Enneatype Conference, sponsored by Parabol Magazine, Lisa Ruyter studio, Vienna

Transpedagogy Symposium (organizer), The Museum of Modern Art, New York; Serpentine Gallery, London (with Sally Tallant)

Illustration Credits

pp. v, ix, x, 4, 6, 11, 20–26, 41, 43, 47, 58, 61, 62 (top and bottom), 63–65, 90, 136, 153, 154, 156, 159. Courtesy Pablo Helguera Archive, New York City

p. 2. Engraving by Cornelius Huyberts. from Frederik Ruysch. *Opera Omnia Anatomico-Medico-Chirurgica. Huc usque edita. Quorum Elenchus pagina sequenti exhibetur. Cum figuris aeneis*. Amsterdam: apud Janssonio-Waesbergios, 1721

p. 7. Portrait of Andreas Vesalius. In Andreas Vesalius' *De Corporis Humani Fabrica*, 1555

p. 9. Anonymous engraving of an anatomy lesson taking place at the Leiden Anatomy Theatre (1609) after a drawing by J. C. vant Woudt (Woudanus)

p. 14. Rembrandt Harmensz van Rijn (1606–1669) *The Anatomy Lesson of Dr. Nicolaes Tulp*, 1632. Oil on canvas, 170 × 217 cm (67 × 85 in.). Courtesy Erich Lessing, Art Resource, New York

p. 16. Rembrandt Harmensz van Rijn (1606–1669). *The Anatomy Lesson of Dr. Joan Deijman*. 1657. Amsterdams Historisch Museum

p. 38. Program of Florence Foster Jenkins's recital at Carnegie Hall, 1944. Courtesy Carnegie Hall Library, New York

p. 45. Jack E. Boucher. *Spiral Stairs.* Shaker Centre Family Trustees' Office, South side of Village Road, North of U.S. Route 68, Pleasant Hill, Mercer County, KY. Documentation compiled after 1933. Collection: Historic American Buildings Survey (Library of Congress)

p. 49. Portrait of Friedrich Fröbel (Frederick Froebel). Lithograph. Syracuse, N.Y.: C.W. Bardeen, Publisher, c. 1897. Courtesy Library of Congress, Prints & Photographs Division

p. 50. Lithograph after Karl Friedrich Schinkel, 1875; *The Arrival of the Queen of the Night*. Stage set for Mozart's *The Magic Flute*. Courtesy Snark, Art Resource, New York

p. 52. Frederick Froebel. Illustration from *Mutter und Kofe-lieder* (*Mother-Play and Nursery Songs*) by Frederick Froebel, 1844

p. 53. Kindergarten dance. Courtesy Deutsches Bundesarchiv (German Federal Archive), Bild 183-26594-0009 (1954-09-27). Author: Weiss

p. 55. Portrait of Ward Jackson. Courtesy the Solomon R. Guggenheim Museum, New York

pp. 96, 128. Photographs of the performance of *The Foreign Legion* at Performa 05, New York, 2005. © Michael Sherman

p. 134. Portrait of Captain George Wellington Streeter. Courtesy Chicago History Museum, Chicago Illinois

www.ingramcontent.com/pod-product-compliance
Lightning Source LLC
LaVergne TN
LVHW090943080826
845145LV00003B/869

* 9 7 8 1 9 3 4 9 7 8 1 6 0 *